# The Medicus® PureStrike™ Golf Swing
*5 Simple Keys to Consistently Striking it Pure*

Finally a quick and easy way for anyone to learn tour proven fundamentals that every great ball striker uses.

ISBN 978-1-938653-11-7

# Table of Contents

# Introduction

At Medicus, we know that very intelligent people often play very poor golf. But we know why: They lack the necessary information they need to improve.

Golf instruction today is full of personal opinions about the swing. It makes you question whether there are any definable truths (facts) in golf on which to rely — or whether you really are doomed to visit instructor after instructor until you find a "method" that works for you.

We're here to prove that great golf swings are not based on guesswork. They rely on definable facts and have several critically important traits in common. The *Medicus® PureStrike™ Golf Swing*, will demystify golf by outlining those common features and show you how to build them into your own game. You'll have no choice but to improve.

## 5 Simple Keys and Educated Hands

The *Medicus® PureStrike™ Golf Swing* is not a single system into which everyone must fit. Rather, it's a universal, science-based system that is adaptable to everyone, regardless of physical characteristics or current skill level.

The *Medicus® PureStrike™ Golf Swing* is built on the fact that all successful golf swings maintain a simple set of highly interdependent Keys. The swings of most PGA Tour professionals are all slightly different — in fact, no two swings on the planet are exactly alike and nobody's is perfect — but the Keys are the same.

The 5 Simple Keys, which we'll soon explain in detail, are:

- Steady Head
- Weight Forward
- Flat Left Wrist
- Sweetspot Path
- Clubface Control

The term "key" suggests that something is essential and foundational. That's exactly what these five Keys are — they're the base on which you build your swing, and they're non-negotiable.

You're probably used to "keys" being things like grip, stance, and ball position. This is backward. Unlike the 5 Simple Keys, your grip, stance, and ball position are actually quite negotiable and can be modified — with no harm done to your swing — based on personal preference.

For example, the grips of good players vary, both in terms of style (overlapping versus interlocking) and orientation on the club (hands turned far to the left versus far to the right). Likewise, some players use a slightly open or slightly closed stance. So, what you think of today as "keys" or "fundamentals" are really nothing of the sort.

The 5 Simple Keys of the *Medicus® PureStrike™ Golf Swing* are the real elements that exist — in pure, non-personalized form — in every great golf swing.

There is a common thread connecting each of the 5 Simple Keys: Your hands.

Your hands are the intermediary between your brain and the club, and they must undergo effective training in order to produce — and reproduce — the five Simple Keys. We call this training process "educating your hands," since the end result is a pair of Educated Hands.

The Keys and Educated Hands form the core of the *Medicus® PureStrike™ Golf Swing*. They're your ticket to better chips, pitches, and full swings, and ultimately to lower scores.

**What to Expect**
The *Medicus® PureStrike™ Golf Swing* takes a straightforward, yet comprehensive, approach to building your golf swing. Each chapter builds on the previous one, so it's important that you read the chapters in order.

We'll start with the "why" — delving further into Educated Hands; the roles that your body, arms, and hands play in the swing; and the 5 Simple Keys.

Then, using what you've learned, we'll tackle the "how" — building your golf swing from the ground up using the techniques we've found to be easiest and most effective for most players. We'll first go through chipping, pitching, and the full swing, as those three motions neatly build right on top of each other.

The knowledge you'll gain from the *Medicus® PureStrike™ Golf Swing* will allow you to continually self-diagnose your game. When you run into problems with your swing, you'll be armed with the information necessary to identify your faults and correct them — no more relying on band-aid fixes that treat your symptoms but fail to solve your true underlying problems.

**Final Thoughts**

The golf swing and the game of golf itself, though a little complex, are actually not very difficult or physically demanding. Additionally, the golf ball is non-discriminatory — it only reacts to the instructions it's given during the fleeting moment of impact and does not care about your gender, age, size, or shape.

Given this, we strongly believe that anyone can achieve a single-digit handicap if five to 10 hours each week are devoted to training and learning. We also believe that the process for building your golf swing is no different than the approach you'd take to learn to drive a car, brush your teeth, or play a guitar. Golf is a step-by-step process toward an identifiable goal: improving to the highest level of your ability.

With that said, remember that growth is an uneven process. Progress rarely follows a straight, upward path. Keep a positive mindset, and don't get too alarmed or frustrated by occasional plateaus or regressions.

Let's get started!

# Educated Hands

An emphasis on "educating the hands" sets the *Medicus® PureStrike™ Golf Swing* apart from other golf instruction books.

Regardless of how many hours you spend on the practice tee hitting balls, you'll achieve only fleeting success without Educated Hands. This lack of success inevitably sends you in search of more information, which only makes golf more confusing and frustrating.

There is only one way for information to travel from your brain to the club and back to your brain, and that's through your hands. Why? Your hands are the only part of your body attached to the club during a golf swing.

Throughout the *Medicus® PureStrike™ Golf Swing*, you'll find drills aimed at improving the ability of your hands to execute skillful, coordinated movements (also known as developing your "manual dexterity"). In golf, having great manual dexterity means having Educated Hands, and the drills in this book will teach you to develop your own set of Educated Hands.

The challenge facing most golfers is that they do not understand — and therefore are unable to feel and produce — the hand assignments necessary to consistently hit great shots. The solution is to train and educate your hands so they know precisely what they're supposed to do.

The process of educating your hands for golf is no different than the training your hands must go through before you find it easy to perform everyday tasks, such as tying your shoes. A surgeon can read everything ever written about how to perform an appendectomy, but until he's able to begin working on real patients, his hands are no better trained to perform the surgery than are your hands.

### Why monitor your hands?
Most golfers attempt to monitor the clubface and try to manipulate it during the swing, all without Educated Hands. This is the opposite of what should be happening. The clubface cannot control your hands, but your hands can control the clubface; likewise, your hands can be trained, but the clubface cannot. Educated Hands are able to achieve the Keys necessary to make good golf-like motions, which when executed on the course lead to good golf.

Another benefit of monitoring and educating your hands is that while the clubhead may be traveling at 100 miles per hour during your swing, your hands will be traveling at just 20 miles per hour. It isn't humanly possible to monitor the clubhead as it streaks through impact, but you can monitor your slower-moving hands.

**Educated Hands Training**
Once you have learned the mechanics of a particular motion, such as a chip, the best way to practice hand education is to do so with your eyes closed. For example, if you want to get a glass off a nearby table, you'd just reach over and grab it. With your eyes open, your focus is on the glass, not your hands. But if you try to perform this same task with your eyes closed, you immediately become very conscious of how your hands move toward and ultimately pick up the glass.

Our students often ask, "How long will it take to educate my hands?" Since everyone is different, we can't offer a definitive answer — but we do know that students quickly begin to start seeing changes in how they think and how they visualize their swings once they begin focusing on Educated Hands. With time and practice, students break the old habits they've created.

You must be methodical and deliberate when educating and training your hands. As your hands become more educated, your focus can shift from training them to simply monitoring them.

**What does it mean to have Educated Hands?**
When you have Educated Hands, you can reliably produce the 5 Simple Keys, which enables you to achieve solid impact and maximize distance and accuracy. Educated Hands also consistently reach Impact Hand Location, where your left wrist is facing the target and your hands are directly underneath your left shoulder.

With Educated Hands, you can immediately tell whether or not you've produced the 5 Simple Keys, which empowers you to troubleshoot your swing on both the practice tee and the course.

Finally, when you have Educated Hands, you know the precise route your hands need to take from - address to the top - to impact - to the finish for any particular length of swing.

Now, while extremely important, Educated Hands are not enough — your arms and body play key roles in transporting your hands during the swing, something you'll learn about in the next chapter.

# Anatomy of the Golf Swing

Right at the outset of this book, we want to provide you with a basic understanding of how the human body functions in a golf swing. There is a lot of confusion in the golf world about "what does what" in a swing.

You can divide the human body into three sections: Body, Arms, and Hands. These sections, which can also be envisioned as layers, build upon one another to create the swing. Each section has multiple parts, as you'll see, and each part has a specific role during the swing.

Although we divide the human body up into these sections, it's important to remember that the golf swing is a unified motion that simultaneously engages parts from all three sections. Thinking of the swing as a collection of parts is fine when you're troubleshooting a problem on the practice tee, but you should never bring this thinking to the course. When you're out playing, it's imperative that you envision your swing as a unified package, or else you're certain to be confused and paralyzed by swing thoughts when you set up to a shot.

**Role of the Body**
The overall role of the body, *known as the pivot*, in the golf swing is to provide support and balance to the motion of the arms and hands. Among many other important things, the pivot transports the hands while also supporting Clubface Control and the application of power (through the arms), both of which we'll explain in more detail later on.

Like a house, your golf swing can only be as good as its foundation. The stable foundation for your golf swing is provided by your body. Without foundational support from a trained pivot, your golf swing will lack stability.

Also, your Educated Hands rely heavily on your pivot. Even if your hands are educated and know where they need to go during the swing, they can only get there if your pivot is properly trained to take them there. A poorly functioning pivot will throw even the most educated set of hands off their correct route.

Let's take a look at what the five major body parts do during the swing, starting with your head and working down.

- **Head.** Your head provides a central point around which you turn your body. It's not the center of the swing (your left shoulder is), but rather the center of the pivot. Your head's job is to remain as steady as possible throughout the swing (the Steady Head, one of the 5 Simple Keys).

Head at address.

Head at the top.

Head at follow-through.

Head at the finish.

- **Shoulders.** Of your two shoulders, your right shoulder is the crucial one. It not only provides guidance to the direction and delivery of your hands into impact, but also — through its rotational motion in the backswing and downswing — applies power by propelling your left arm off your chest. The faster you rotate your right shoulder in the downswing, the farther you'll hit the ball.

Shoulders are parallel to your target line at address

Shoulders have turned 90° around your spine at the top.

Right shoulder points at your target line at follow-though.

Shoulders at the finish.

- **Hips.** Your hips are a facilitator, as they make it possible for your hands to move in a straight line from the top to impact. Your hips do this by sliding slightly toward the target as the downswing begins, creating room for your right elbow and your hands to take a direct path to the ball. Improper hip action will result in your right elbow colliding with your right hip (or you'll instinctively reroute your right elbow around your hip), which prevents you from moving your hands in a straight line between the top and impact.

Hips at address.

Hips in the backswing.

Hips at startdown.

Hips at the finish.

- **Knees.** Your knees and hips help keep your head steady and centered throughout the swing. At the top, your left knee has become slightly more bent than it was at address, while your right knee has become slightly straighter.

  In the downswing, both knees regain nearly the same flex they had at address. Then, as you approach impact, your left knee begins to straighten while your right knee remains slightly bent. At the finish, your left knee is straight or nearly straight, and your right knee remains slightly bent.

  Though your knee flex changes slightly during the swing, excessively changing it will raise or lower your head — a fault known as bobbing — which in turn disrupts a number of Keys and makes it very difficult to hit consistent shots.

Knees at address.

Knees at the top.

Knees in the downswing.

Knees at impact.

Knees at the finish.

- **Feet.** Your feet are the true foundation of your swing. They act like anchors, keeping you grounded while supporting all the rotation and thrust that's going on up above with your shoulders and arms. At address and in the backswing, both feet are relatively flat.

  As you approach impact, your left foot stays flat while you begin to roll onto the inside of your right foot. Your right foot continues to roll until the finish, at which point your right heel is off the ground with only your right toe touching the ground.

Feet at address.

Feet at the top.

Feet approaching impact.

Feet at follow-through.

Feet at the finish.

**Role of the Arms**

In your golf swing, your arms provide support to the clubshaft and generate power. Though many believe the body provides the swing's power, it's in fact the arms that do so. Which can you do faster, turn your body or swing your arms? Of course, the answer is "swing your arms."

As with the body (pivot), the motion of your arms is controlled and enhanced by your Educated Hands. Once your arms are properly trained, it's your Educated Hands that are responsible for moving them during the swing and giving them precision.

- **Left Arm.** Your left arm moves across your chest in the backswing, which puts it in position to be blasted off your chest during the downswing. It must stay straight from address to follow-through — follow-through is the point when both arms are straight after impact with the club at a 45° angle to the ground — after which it folds to the finish.

  Your left arm provides power during the swing in two ways: as it swings back and forth, and as it rotates to the right and left. At impact, it must be perpendicular to the ground (directly underneath your left shoulder).

Left arm at address.

Left arm at the top.

Left arm at the top
(down-the-line view).

Left arm at impact.

Left arm at follow-through.

Left arm at the finish.

- **Right Arm.** Your right arm fans, folds, straightens into follow-through, and then (depending on the shot) remains straight or is bent at the finish. As your right arm bends and straightens, it provides power itself while also automatically cocking and uncocking your left wrist, which also contributes power.

Right arm at address.

Right arm in the backswing.

Right arm at the top.                    Right arm at follow-through.

Right arm at the finish.

Your right forearm, as a portion of your right arm, controls the clubshaft and points directly at your target line from the time it moves beyond parallel to the ground in the downswing until you reach follow-through. In doing so, it acts like a brace to support the clubshaft during impact.

Right forearm parallel to the
ground in the downswing.

Right forearm pointing at target
line as impact is approached.

Right forearm still pointing at
target line at follow-through.

**Role of the Hands**

Given that we dedicated the entire first chapter of the *Medicus
PureStrike™ Golf Swing* to the concept of Educated Hands, you've
probably realized that the hands are the golf swing's "command center"
and extremely critical to playing great golf. In fact, we'll say that you're
not able to consistently play great golf unless you've trained your hands
properly.

Your hands are responsible for executing shots, controlling the golf ball, and creating precision in your pivot. In addition to being your overall "command center," each hand (and wrist) has a specific role to play.

- **Left Hand and Wrist.** Your left hand and wrist are responsible for Clubface Control (one of the 5 Simple Keys discussed later) by providing the proper clubface motion. The other critical role for your left hand and wrist is linking your left arm and the clubshaft, essentially locking them into one straight line (a radius). Finally, as mentioned previously, your left wrist cocks and uncocks during the swing - which provides some power - as a result of your right arm bending and straightening.

Left wrist at address (uncocked).       Left wrist at the top (cocked).

Left arm and clubshaft in a straight line at impact (radius of the swing), linked by the Flat Left Wrist.

- **Right Hand and Wrist.** Your right hand and wrist control the clubhead. Your right wrist's main job is to remain frozen in a bent position from the top to follow-through; at address, it can be either bent or flat. As you'll learn more about, the first joint of your right index finger is responsible for monitoring the clubhead's sweetspot and delivering it to the ball at impact.

Right wrist bent at address.        Right wrist bent at impact.

- **Both Hands as a Unit.** Both hands have a critical role at impact — they must arrive at Impact Hand Location. This means they are directly underneath your left shoulder while appearing from your point of view to be over the toes of your left foot, and they've rotated so your left wrist is facing the target.

By knowing that your hands must reach Impact Hand Location, you're well on your way to getting them there. Almost all golfers are unaware of where their hands need to be at impact, which certainly makes it difficult to get them to the proper location.

Both hands slightly behind left
shoulder at address.

Both hands directly underneath left
shoulder at impact.

We recommend that you spend most of your practice time training
your left and right hands to produce and reproduce the Keys that we'll
discuss next. Educated Hands can compensate, to some extent, for faults
elsewhere in the swing — they're like insurance. Not only will Educated
Hands empower you to consistently hit good shots, but they'll also make
your misses less severe.

# 5 Simple Keys to Solid Ball Striking

Central to the *Medicus® PureStrike™ Golf Swing* — and all great golf swings — are the 5 Simple Keys, which we'll outline and explain throughout this chapter. Understand, practice, and master these five Keys and you'll gain control over the golf club's three parts — the clubface, clubhead, and clubshaft — and therefore gain control over the golf ball itself.

**The 5 Simple Keys**

- Steady Head
- Weight Forward
- Flat Left Wrist
- Sweetspot Path
- Clubface Control

Unlike most mainstream golf instruction, the *Medicus® PureStrike™ Golf Swing* focuses on alignments, not positions. Alignments trump positions because it's possible to be in every supposedly correct position and still miss the ball due to poor alignments. As long as you comply with the 5 Simple Keys, you can swing the club any way you'd like — though some ways are easier and more effective than others, and we'll cover those later on.

Though each of the Keys are definable and separate, all five are highly interdependent; their cause and effect on each other is tremendous. Improving one has a positive effect on the others, while errors in one compromise your ability to properly execute the others.

Any given Key can only be executed "correctly" or "incorrectly" and nobody perfectly achieves all five Keys on every single swing.

The important thing to keep in mind is that there is a difference between executing a Key "extremely incorrectly" and "slightly incorrectly." You've made progress if you're executing a Key better than you did last month, last week, or yesterday. Over time, your objective is to make each one less and less incorrect until you're able to correctly execute all of them more often than not.

These 5 Simple Keys are found in every swing, from the shortest chip to the longest drive. Though complying with all five is crucial for great golf, we'll introduce them here in order of importance.

## Key #1: Steady Head

**What is a Steady Head and how do I achieve it?**
A Steady Head is a head that stays centered between the feet from address until at least follow-through. During the swing, your head is a fixed point around which you turn back and forth — it does not move from side to side or up and down.

To get a feel for a Steady Head, face a wall and take your address position (without a club) so the top of your forehead is touching the wall. Now, move your hands to the top, impact, and finish as you would during a real swing. This will feel very awkward if you are used to moving your head laterally or vertically during the swing, but it's what a true Steady Head feels like.

**Don't some good players move their heads?**

Yes. As you observe other players, including some PGA Tour professionals, you will undoubtedly see some who move their heads from side to side during the swing and still manage to play good golf.

So while this is an option, we strongly prefer the Steady Head. Why add another moving part to your swing, especially if it contributes nothing to power or accuracy and can only cause problems?

Wall drill at address.

Wall drill at the top.

Wall drill at impact

Wall drill at the finish.

While hitting balls, use your eyes to monitor your Steady Head. When you take your address position, your eyes are fixed on a certain view of the top of the ball. If that view changes during the swing, you know you've disrupted your Steady Head. If your head moves over your back foot during the swing, you'll be looking at the back of the ball instead of the top. If your head moves over your front foot during the swing, you'll be looking at the front of the ball.

Only after follow-through should your head begin rotating around until you're facing the target. If you've swung with a Steady Head, you should be able to maintain your finish position for at least seven seconds.

**Why do I need a Steady Head?**
The Steady Head contributes to your overall balance — keeping you centered over the ball and not inclined to "tip" in any direction — and gives you a much better chance of striking the ball consistently and with precision.

A Steady Head also enables you to achieve proper Impact Hand Location, where your hands are directly underneath your left shoulder and your left wrist is facing the target.

Imagine a camera tripod, but with a 10- to 12-pound bowling ball on top instead of a camera. If you remove or bend one of the three legs, the bowling ball will fall to the ground. Likewise, if the bowling ball drifts too far from the exact center of the three legs, it will no longer be balanced and will fall. Though golfers have only two legs and a tripod has three, moving the head — just like moving the bowling ball — causes imbalance and inconsistency.

**What happens if I don't have a Steady Head?**
Disruption of the Steady Head leads to highly inconsistent contact. When your head moves forward toward the ball, it can lead to shots off the heel or even shanks. When your head moves away from the ball, you'll likely hit thin shots.

When your head moves from side to side, so does your upper body, which means you're altering your ball position relative to your shoulders. For example, when your head is way behind the ball at impact, you've essentially moved the ball forward in your stance, meaning you'll have to manipulate your hands to hit a good shot.

Ball position is between the shoulders at address.

Head has moved over the back foot, moving the ball position forward relative to the shoulders.

Head has moved over the front foot, moving the ball position backward relative to the shoulders.

When your head moves up and down, you're also moving your upper body — including your radius — up and down. To compensate for this, you'll instinctively lunge down toward the ball (if you've moved up) to avoid hitting it thin, or bend your left wrist or left arm (if you've moved down) to avoid hitting it fat.

Head is level at address.

Head has moved down significantly at impact, causing a fat shot.

Head has moved up significantly at impact, causing a topped shot.

**Why do golfers have problems achieving a Steady Head?**
Golfers who disrupt the Steady Head often have misconceptions about how the body and golf club work and what creates power in the golf swing.

Beginners usually try to help the ball into the air — rather than properly striking down on it — and while trying to "hit up" will move their heads up and/or away from the target. Golfers tired of hitting the ball fat (for one reason or another) will instinctively move their heads up in an attempt to make proper contact.

Those who mistakenly believe that the body is responsible for power often try to get their upper body "behind the ball" in the backswing. You're actually already "behind the ball" at address, so any effort to move it further back during the swing will disrupt the Steady Head.

Finally, golfers have long been taught that their weight should be on the balls of their feet at address, when in fact it should be more toward their heels. You're actually pulled slightly toward the ball during the swing, so keeping your weight on your heels allows you to offset that momentum and maintain a Steady Head.

**Steady, Time-Tested Advice**

Long before this book, some of golf's greats were discussing the importance of a Steady Head.

"The first and always the most important of Jack [Grout]'s fundamentals concerned your head. You had to keep it in the same place throughout the swing, not rigidly anchored, but steady."

— Jack Nicklaus describing the teachings of his longtime instructor, Jack Grout, in *My Story*

"Sam [Snead] told me late in his life that his secret was to swing around his head. Sam was the best at keeping his head still."

— Tom Watson in *Golf Digest*

**What's the bottom line?**
As you work on keeping a Steady Head, remember that all progress is good progress. A head that moves 2 inches during the swing is better than one that moves 4 inches — though a head that moves zero inches is best. Keep working incrementally to eliminate head movement until there is no movement at all.

## Key #2: Weight Forward

### What is Weight Forward and how do I achieve it?
Weight Forward means smoothly moving your lower body weight onto your left foot beginning at startdown and continuing until follow-through, all while maintaining a Steady Head. The purpose of Weight Forward is to enable your hands to travel in a straight line from the top to follow-through, passing through Impact Hand Location along the way.

At address head is centered.

At Impact the head stays centered or has moved only slightly forward (towards target).

At address, your lower body weight should be evenly distributed — about 50 percent on each foot. During the backswing, your pivot should turn back sharply with minimal lateral movement. At startdown, your lower body weight begins to move forward — try to feel like you're pressing down firmly on your left foot.

At impact, between 70 and 85 percent of your lower body weight has moved onto your left foot. After impact, your weight continues to move forward — aim to feel a continually increasing pressure on your left foot. At the finish, 90 to 95 percent of your lower body weight should be on your left foot.

Weight Forward is achieved by proper lower body action, particularly that of the knees and hips. At startdown, your left knee and hips slide (or "bump") slightly toward the target, causing your weight to start moving onto your left foot. After this brief slide, your hips begin to turn, placing even more weight on your left foot. Your hips continue turning all the way through to the finish. Without this proper sequence of lower body action, you won't have the necessary 70 to 85 percent of your lower body weight on your left foot at impact.

To get a feel for proper lower body action and Weight Forward, you'll need a chair and a golf tee. Place the chair a couple inches outside of your left hip. Put the tee in the ground about 6 to 7 inches ahead of (and in-line with) the toes of your left foot on the target side, which represents where your hands should arrive — from your line-of-sight perspective — at follow-through (the point when both arms are straight after impact with the club at a 45° angle to the ground).

Make a swing without a club, watching how your left hip has to slide into the chair in the downswing to enable your hands to reach follow-through. Also note how your weight moves onto your left foot as your left hip moves toward the chair.

If you're not used to making a proper hip slide, this is going to feel extreme at first. But, it's the motion that's necessary to achieve Weight Forward and allow your hands to travel in a straight line from the top to follow-through.

Weight is evenly distributed at address.

Pivot turns sharply in the backswing.

Weight begins to move forward in the downswing as the left knee and hips slide slightly toward the target.

At release point, hips have become square to the target as weight has continued to move onto the left foot.

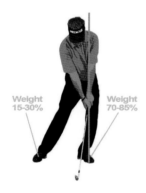

Weight 15-30%
Weight 70-85%

At impact, majority of lower body weight is on the left foot.

## Why do I need Weight Forward?

All the best ball strikers have their Weight Forward — on their left foot — at impact, while all poor ball strikers have their weight on their right foot at impact. There is a direct correlation between the amount of Weight Forward at impact and the handicap of the player. The lower the handicap, the more Weight Forward (and vice versa).

Having Weight Forward helps you strike down on the ball, allowing you to contact the ball first and then the ground. It also promotes solid contact by making it easier for you to have a Flat Left Wrist and your hands ahead of the clubhead at impact. Finally, Weight Forward helps keep the clubhead traveling on the Sweetspot Path, which is essential for consistent ball striking.

### A word from Mr. Hogan

Ben Hogan, who many consider to be one of the best ball strikers ever to play the game, recognized the importance of proper lower body action and Weight Forward.

"The hips initiate the downswing. To begin the downswing, turn your hips back to the left. There must be enough lateral motion forward to transfer the weight to the left foot."

— Ben Hogan in *Five Lessons: The Modern Fundamentals of Golf*

## What happens if I don't have Weight Forward?

Having the majority of your lower body weight on your right foot at impact is the opposite of Weight Forward. A lack of Weight Forward means that you're hanging back on your right side, which makes it nearly impossible for your hands to reach Impact Hand Location. As a result, the clubhead will pass your hands before impact, disrupting the Flat Left Wrist (Key #3) and adding loft to the clubface. You'll end up losing distance and hitting fat and thin shots.

Hanging back on your right side also moves your ball position forward relative to your shoulders. As we'll discuss in the next Key — the Flat Left Wrist — the lowest point of your swing arc is directly below the outside edge of your left shoulder. When you hang back and allow your left shoulder to move away from the target, you'll hit fat shots.

Weight (and head) too far back coming into impact, leading to a fat shot.

Weight (and head) too far forward coming into impact, leading to a thin shot.

Correct Weight Forward and Steady Head at impact.

**Why do golfers have problems achieving Weight Forward?**
The reasons why golfers have trouble achieving Weight Forward are very similar to the reasons why they disrupt the Steady Head.

The most common reason why golfers don't achieve Weight Forward is that they're trying to help the ball get in the air. When you try to "hit up" on the ball — instead of trying to drive it into the ground — you end up with the majority of your lower body weight on your right foot at impact.

Another reason is that players overuse or misuse their knees and lower bodies, and it's oftentimes because they believe it contributes to power (it doesn't). When your lower body is overactive or moves out of sequence, you'll tend to tilt away from the target in the downswing, meaning your lower body weight will remain on your right foot instead of shifting to your left foot.

Overactive upper bodies are also an issue. Some players move their entire body forward in the downswing rather than just their lower body (knees and hips). This upper body "lunge" feels powerful, but is actually powerless.

Finally, players have been taught to get their head "behind the ball." This leads them to try to move their head away from the target during the swing, which prevents lower body weight from moving to the left foot. In reality, your head is already "behind the ball" if you take a proper address position with your head centered between your feet. There's no need to move it anywhere during the swing — if you do, you disrupt both Weight Forward and the Steady Head.

**What's the bottom line?**
Without exception, all good players move their weight onto their left foot in the downswing. They accomplish this through proper lower body action and correct sequencing — the left knee and hips slide to initiate the downswing, after which the hips begin turning and bring the shoulders, arms, hands, and club along for the ride. Get this sequence correct and you set the foundation for solid ball striking.

# Key #3: Flat Left Wrist

## What is the Flat Left Wrist and how do I achieve it?

We define the Flat Left Wrist as a left wrist that is flat — in-line with the left forearm — from at least impact to follow-through (the point when both arms are straight after impact with the club at a 45° angle to the ground).

At some point before impact, you must establish the Flat Left Wrist and lock it into place. This allows you to deliver the entire club, not just the clubhead, into the ball.

Alternatives to "flat" are "bent" (cupped) and "arched" (bowed). Though a slightly arched left wrist is generally not a problem, avoid a bent left wrist at all costs.

### When Training, Err on the Side of "Arched"

Most golfers' left wrists are bent at impact, which leads to all sorts of trouble. So while educating your hands to consistently produce a Flat Left Wrist, you may find it helpful to strive for a slightly arched left wrist.

A left wrist that's slightly arched provides some "insurance" against the dangers of a bent left wrist.

The only negative byproduct of a slightly arched left wrist is that the ball will tend to fly a bit right of your target.

Bent           Arched          Flat

## Why do I need the Flat Left Wrist?

The Flat Left Wrist controls the clubface and is the number one alignment in golf. The absence of the Flat Left Wrist is the most common problem among golfers and absolutely destroys golf swings.

The Flat Left Wrist is also your gateway to creating the *radius of the swing*. In geometry, a radius is a line from the center of a circle to its perimeter. In terms of the golf swing, the radius is the straight line formed by your left arm, the Flat Left Wrist, and the clubshaft. The radius begins at your left shoulder — the center of your swing arc — and extends to the lowest point of your swing arc, which you can think of as the end of your divot.

The radius, which is responsible for applying power and ensuring solid contact, must be in place from at least impact (where it is approximately perpendicular to the ground, directly underneath your left shoulder) to follow-through. The critical link between your straight left arm and the clubshaft is the Flat Left Wrist, as a left wrist that's bent, or excessively arched, means the radius is bent too.

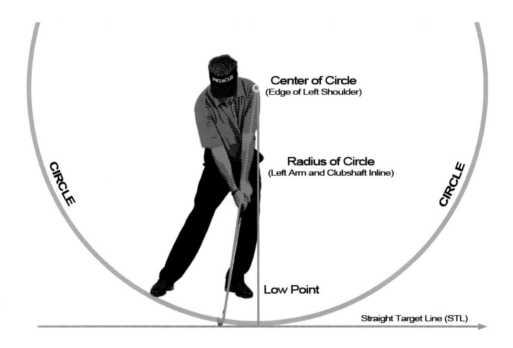

Geometry of the golf swing.

**What happens if I don't have the Flat Left Wrist?**
If you disrupt the Flat Left Wrist, you unleash a domino effect. First, you've lost Clubface Control (Key #5) so expect to have erratic and improper club face motion, which leads to hitting fat, thin, and topped

shots. Additionally, bending your left wrist creates a radius that's bent — rather than in a straight line — while also throwing the clubhead off its proper plane and path, leading to inaccurate shots and robbing you of distance.

Bent left wrist causing a topped shot.

Bent left wrist causing a thin shot.

Bent left wrist causing a fat shot.

**Why do golfers have problems achieving the Flat Left Wrist?**
Flattening the right wrist — which disrupts the Flat Left Wrist — comes naturally to most people. When throwing a baseball or shooting a basketball, your right wrist goes from bent to flat to arched as the ball leaves your hand and you complete your follow-through. This is exactly what we don't want to do in golf. In golf, your right wrist must stay bent back from at least impact to follow-through.

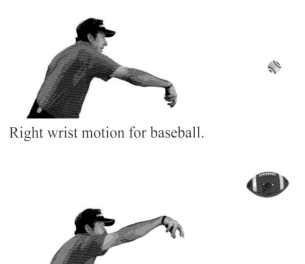

Right wrist motion for baseball.

Right wrist motion for football.

Right wrist motion for basketball.

Also, players are often under the impression that impact alignments are the same as address alignments, and that at impact the club should be returned to its address position. Unless you deliberately take your address position for all shots with the clubshaft leaning toward the target and your left wrist flat — which we do recommend for chip shots — your hands and clubshaft at impact should look nothing like they do at address.

At address, you have the option of starting with your hands in the center of your body, your left wrist is slightly bent, and the clubshaft is vertical - or, as a lot of players do, you can start with the club soled as it was designed, with the clubshaft leaning slightly forward and the grip end of the club pointing to the inside part of your left thigh.

Regardless of how you set up, at impact your hands are ahead of the clubhead, your left wrist is flat, and the clubshaft is leaning toward the target.

Though they don't know it, most players sign up for golf lessons so they can fix problems with their left hands and left wrists.

**What's the bottom line?**
Your task, regardless of your skill level, is to ensure you can produce and reproduce the Flat Left Wrist. Nothing works if you bend your left wrist.

If you take nothing else from this chapter, remember that having the Flat Left Wrist from at least impact to follow-through is the most important alignment in golf, and that the Flat Left Wrist is a product of having Educated Hands.

## Key #4: Sweetspot Path

### What is the Sweetspot Path and how do I get on it?

As the clubface approaches the golf ball, it travels on an angle — not along your target line. We call this angle the Sweetspot Path because it's the line on top of which the clubface's sweetspot travels into impact.

The sweetspot is the pinhead-sized point on the clubface where the ball is most effectively and efficiently struck, which in turn maximizes both distance and accuracy.

### How do I locate the Sweetspot?

The sweetspot of a given clubface can be found using a piece of string or a thin dowel.

While holding the string or dowel up against the right side of the grip, hold both out in front of you and let them hang vertically.

You may have expected the dowel or string to hang down along the clubshaft, but it doesn't. Instead, it intersects the clubface, passing through the sweetspot along the way.

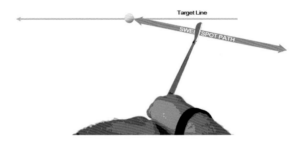

Sweetspot approaching impact.

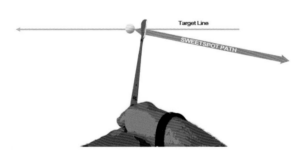

Sweetspot just before impact.

After impact, the sweetspot begins moving down your target line and then moves back to the inside.

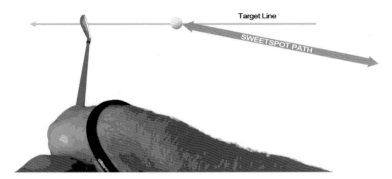

Sweetspot at follow-through.

The best way to ensure you get on the Sweetspot Path is to monitor *sweetspot pressure*, which is the feeling of the clubface's sweetspot trailing your hands. Sweetspot pressure is sensed through the first joint of your right hand index finger (your "trigger finger"), a pressure point that sits on the back side of the grip.

Location of pressure point.                    Pressure point against the grip.

You'll start to feel a strong increase in sweetspot pressure — a heavy, dragging feeling — as you change direction at the top from the backswing to the downswing. Your goal is to steadily increase this pressure as you drive it down to the inside rear portion of the ball. If you successfully do this, you'll be on the Sweetspot Path every time you swing the club.

Red dot indicates the point on the ball where the Sweetspot Pressure, and therefore the sweetspot, is to be directed.

**Why do I need to be on the Sweetspot Path?**

When you're on the Sweetspot Path and have heavy sweetspot pressure, you're ensuring that the clubface's sweetspot — not the heel, toe, or another part of the clubface — is being delivered to the ball. This results in a solid impact and maximizes distance and accuracy.

Being on the Sweetspot Path also guarantees that you're on plane and have correctly achieved a number of other Keys, including the Flat Left Wrist.

**What happens if I'm not on the Sweetspot Path?**

Not being on the Sweetspot Path means the clubface's sweetspot is off plane, which leads to shots low on the face, high on the face, and off the heel and toe. You may even hit shanks. Likewise, approaching impact on an angle other than the Sweetspot Path means you're delivering the sweetspot somewhere other than the inside rear portion of the ball, which affects accuracy.

To ensure this doesn't happen, you must be diligent about aiming your sweetspot pressure (via the first joint of your right hand index finger) toward the inside rear part of the ball. You must also constantly check your grip to confirm that the first joint of your right hand index finger is behind — not on top of or underneath — the grip.

Sweetspot pressure aimed toward the inside rear part of the ball at the top.

**Why do golfers have problems getting on the Sweetspot Path?**
As with Clubface Control, most golfers have never heard of the Sweetspot Path, which certainly makes it difficult for them to cover it with the clubhead.

In addition, many golfers believe they must deliberately throw the clubhead at the ball as they approach impact. As you've learned, this type of action not only disrupts the Sweetspot Path but also the Flat Left Wrist. Rather than throwing the clubhead at the ball, you should focus on driving your sweetspot pressure through the ball and down into the ground.

**What's the bottom line?**
Delivering the clubface's sweetspot into impact along the Sweetspot Path is the only way to ensure that you consistently hit the golf ball on the sweetspot of the clubface, which maximizes accuracy and distance. And the more sweetspot pressure you can deliver to the ball, the more power you'll deliver.

# Key #5: Clubface Control

**What is Clubface Control and how do I achieve it?**
Clubface Control is the ability to execute the correct *Clubface Motion* (movement of the clubface) from startup through follow-through. You apply a Clubface Motion in every swing you make, so you'll always apply some sort of Clubface Motion — what's imperative is that you apply the Clubface Motion required for the particular shot you need to hit.

As mentioned earlier, the Flat Left Wrist controls the clubface, so it should make sense that your clubface motion is controlled by how your Flat Left Wrist moves during the swing.

There are three Clubface Motions that you can apply during a swing: A, B, and C. Each one produces a slightly different trajectory, though all of them can produce a straight ball flight.

You can determine which one of them you applied during a particular swing by examining where the clubface's leading edge is pointing at follow-through. Plan to check the clubface only when taking less-than-full swings, as you're moving too fast to stop at follow-through during a full swing.

As you begin to train your hands (remember our ongoing emphasis on educating your hands?) to produce the three Clubface Motions, you'll also start learning what each one "feels like" to you. For example, what difference do you feel in the motion your Flat Left Wrist is making during the swing as you produce Clubface Motion A versus Clubface Motion B?

The three Clubface Motions are:

- **Clubface Motion A.** The clubface opens in the backswing and closes in the downswing; it's like a saloon door opening and closing. Clubface Motion A is normally used in full swings, and it's what you'll naturally apply during a full swing if you don't interfere (by trying to steer the clubhead, for example) with your left wrist motion. To verify that you've applied Clubface Motion A, stop your swing at follow-through — the clubface's leading edge should be pointing about 70° to 80° across your target line (nearly parallel to the line, but not quite).

Clubface Motion A.

- **Clubface Motion B.** The clubface opens slightly in the backswing and closes while laying back (toward the sky) in the downswing. Clubface Motion B is normally used for short shots. To verify that you've applied Clubface Motion B, stop your swing at follow-through — the clubface's leading edge should be pointing 45° across your target line.

Clubface Motion B.

- **Clubface Motion C.** The clubface stays facing the ball in the backswing and lays back (toward the sky) in the downswing; it's like a pet door opening and closing. Clubface Motion C is used for specialty pitch shots like lob shots. To verify that you've applied Clubface Motion C, stop your swing at follow-through — the clubface's leading edge should be perpendicular to your target line with the clubface facing the sky.

Clubface Motion C.

**Why do I need proper Clubface Control?**
Clubface Control is responsible for a shot's accuracy. Being able to consistently apply the correct clubface motion you intended will give you a consistent ball flight.

**What happens if I don't have proper Clubface Control?**
If, for a given shot, you intend to use the clubface like a door (Clubface Motion A) but don't close the door (the clubface) enough before impact, the ball will go right. If you close it too much, you'll hit it left. Clubface Motion, through the Flat Left Wrist, is what allows you to control where the ball goes.

**Why do golfers have problems achieving proper Clubface Control?**
Most golfers have never heard of Clubface Control or clubface motion

and don't know that the Flat Left Wrist controls the clubface. Also, many golfers disrupt the Flat Left Wrist — for example, by "throwing" the clubhead at the ball near impact or trying to "help" the ball into the air — which causes erratic clubface behavior and eliminates any chance of applying the clubface motion that was intended for a particular shot.

**What's the bottom line?**
Being able to consistently apply the clubface motion you intend is a product of having Educated Hands. Train your Flat Left Wrist to produce and reproduce each of the three Clubface Motions while learning the differences between how each one "feels" as you produce it.

# Building Your Golf Swing

Let's begin building your golf swing from the ground up. We'll start with chipping, after which we'll move on to pitching, and finally the full swing. These three motions build directly on top of each other. You might be tempted to skip chipping and pitching and go directly to the full swing but be aware that training the three motions in the sequence we've presented is the easiest and most effective way to develop Educated Hands and learn the 5 Simple Keys.

## Chipping

As you build your golf swing from the ground up and learn to execute the five Keys using Educated Hands, chipping is the first motion you must master. You'll utilize chip shots when you're fewer than about 6 feet off the green, such as on the fringe or in very light rough. For most chip shots, the clubhead won't move more than about 2 feet back and 2 feet through.

Chipping begins to educate and train your hands as to where they must be at impact — directly underneath your left shoulder with your Flat Left Wrist facing the target, which we call *Impact Hand Location*. If you can't consistently arrive at Impact Hand Location during a 2-foot chipping motion, imagine how hard it will be in a full swing where the clubhead moves about 20 feet.

In addition, chipping is a great way to learn how the initial startup of the golf club should be performed. You'll simply build on this motion as we continue into pitches and full swings.

Some important concepts to keep in mind while chipping:

- **Remember the Keys and Educated Hands.** As with all swings, your chipping motion must be guided by your Educated Hands and comply with all five Keys.

- **Clubface is king.** It's imperative that you strike the ball with a square clubface. For chipping, you'll be using Clubface Motion B, which means the clubface will open and close slightly during the motion, but you may feel as though the clubface isn't doing anything at all.

- **Get the ball rolling.** A chip has minimal air time and maximal ground time. Once a chip shot lands on the green, it should roll toward the hole just like a putt would.

- **The intermediate target.** This is a point, such as a discolored blade of grass, an old ball mark, or the edge of a divot, that lies on your target line about 6 to 12 inches ahead of the ball. Consider this your target now rather than the hole; the ball should fly over this target after it leaves the clubface.

- **Landing spot stays consistent.** Regardless of how far the distance is between your ball and the hole, your target landing spot is one pace onto the green (about one yard). Your choice of club dictates the roll distance to the hole.

- **To vary distance, vary clubs.** To control distance, don't change your chipping motion or Keys — change the club you're using. The club you choose will dictate how far the ball rolls after landing on the green. A chip with an 8 iron will roll farther than a chip with a pitching wedge.

- **Try to make it.** Give chips the same attention and focus you give to putts. Your goal is to make the chip, not just get it close — though all your misses should stop within 3 feet of the hole.

**Pre-shot**

Remind yourself what you intend to do: Get the ball on the green and let it roll toward the hole like a putt. Choose the appropriate club based on the distance of the chip. Your target line — an imaginary straight line that extends from the ball to the target — will serve as your guide while chipping.

To find your intermediate target, hold the club up in front of you so that the ball and the target are in-line with the clubshaft, creating a straight line between the ball and the target.

Now, lower the club until you find a spot about 6 to 12 inches in front of the ball that you'll be able to see out of your peripheral vision once you take your address position. This spot is called your intermediate target, and it's where you should aim your clubface at address.

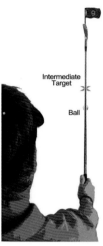

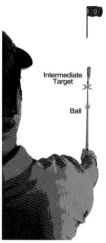

Create a straight line between the ball and target.

Lower the club until you find your intermediate target.

**Grip**

The grip you use for chipping will be identical to the one you'll use for pitching and the full swing. To take your chipping grip:

- Hold the club out in front of you and level to the ground. Place the club on the heel pad of your left hand and close your fingers around the grip.

Place the club on the heel pad of your left hand.

Close your fingers around the grip.

- Add your right hand to the club so that your left thumb fits between the grip and the "lifeline" of your right palm. Connect your right hand to your left hand using an overlapping, interlocking, or 10-finger (baseball) grip style.

Add your right hand to the club.

- Close your right hand around your left thumb and grip, ensuring that the first joint of your right hand index finger (your "trigger" finger) is on the back side of (not on top of or underneath) the grip so you can monitor sweetspot pressure for getting on Sweetspot Path.

Proper grip.

**Setup and Address**

Setting up properly to a chip shot ensures you have the best chance of striking the little ball (the golf ball) before the big ball (the Earth). Regardless of golf ability, anyone can get into an address position that looks as good as any professional player. It takes absolutely no athletic ability to set up correctly to a golf ball, so work diligently on your posture, stance, and hand and ball position until you can consistently set up properly.

• **Posture.** Begin by standing up straight with your feet several inches apart. Lean your upper body (your spine) slightly toward the target, placing about 70 to 80 percent of your weight on your left side. This allows you to establish your Weight Forward prior to beginning the swing. Ensure your head is over your left foot — this is the only shot in golf where we do not recommend starting with your head in the center of your feet, though it should still stay steady throughout the motion. Then, bend forward from your hips and slightly flex your knees.

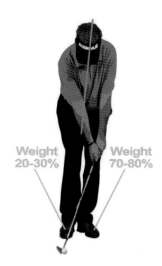

Proper posture with Weight Forward.

- **Stance.** Your stance can be square or slightly open.

Proper stance.

- **Hands.** Place your hands in-line with your left thigh, which tilts the clubshaft slightly toward the target and establishes the Flat Left Wrist. The clubface should be square to your intermediate target.

Proper hand position.

- **Ball Position.** The ball should be back of center, about in-line with the big toe of your right foot.

Proper ball position.

**Making the Motion**

First and foremost, strive to achieve all 5 Simple Keys in every chip you hit.

A proper chipping motion feels just like clapping. Without a club, take an address position. Keeping your body, left arm, and left hand motionless, swing your right forearm and hand back until you reach your right thigh — we call this "fanning" your right forearm — and then swing forward until your right palm hits your left palm. Let momentum take your hands forward to follow-through. Try to recreate this feel with a club in your hands and no ball, and then add a ball and recreate the feel when hitting real chip shots.

Clapping at address.

Clapping at the top.

Clapping at follow-through.

- **Startup and Backswing.** Make the fanning motion (as just described) with your right forearm to start the club back, keeping the clubhead moving along the Sweetspot Path.

Startup and Backswing.

- **Top.** At the end of your backswing, your left arm has moved slightly across your chest — creating a small amount of pressure between your left arm and chest — and your hands are in-line with your right thigh. Your left arm and the clubshaft are in a straight line. You still have a Flat Left Wrist and the clubface has turned slightly open, but not as a result of you deliberately opening it. Your head has not moved from its address position (Steady Head).

Top.

- **Startdown and Downswing.** Turn your right shoulder toward the inside rear part of the ball, which in turn drives your hands toward the inside rear part of the ball. You'll feel an increase in the dragging sensation of sweetspot pressure on the first joint of your right hand index finger. Continue directing this toward the inside rear part of the ball which allows you to get on Sweetspot Path.

Downswing.

- **Impact.** Your hands are at Impact Hand Location (appearing to you to be over the toes of your left foot, with your Flat Left Wrist facing the target). The clubface, which opened very slightly in the backswing, has closed as a result of you reaching Impact Hand Location and is

56

now square to the target. You've driven your accumulated sweetspot pressure into the inside rear part of the ball.

Impact.

- **Follow-through (also serves as your finish).** You've driven through impact and both arms are now straight. Your Flat Left Wrist has continued to link your left arm and the clubshaft in a straight line — your radius. The clubface has continued to close and is pointing about 45° across your target line which means you've correctly utilized Clubface Motion B and have Clubface Control.

Follow-through.
Motion B

Clubface.

**Drills**
These drills can be done at the course or at home, and with a ball or without a ball. The first one should even be done without a club.

- **Clapping Drill (for chipping)**
  *Purpose:* To educate your hands as to the feel of a proper chipping motion.
  *Equipment:* Just your hands.
  *Instructions:* Take an address position. Keeping your body, left arm, and left hand motionless, swing your right arm and hand back until you reach your right thigh (a fanning motion). Then, while maintaining the backward bend in the right wrist, swing forward until your right palm hits your left palm. Allow momentum to bring you to follow-through (both arms straight after impact).

**Quick Tips: Chipping**

- Ball position is back of center to ensure a downward strike
- Weight favors your left side
- Hands and wrists remain passive, with the Flat Left Wrist intact
- Left arm and clubshaft stay in a straight line during the entire motion
- Change clubs, not the motion, for longer chips

Clapping Drill at address.

Clapping Drill at the top.

Clapping Drill at follow-through.

Poor golfers, rather than finishing with both palms touching, drive the fingers of their right hand into their left palm, which disrupts the Flat Left Wrist.

Clapping Drill done incorrectly.

- **2x4 Drill (for chipping)**
  *Purpose:* To educate your hands to execute a chipping motion with proper clubface alignment and clubhead path.
  *Equipment:* A club, two 2x4s, a golf ball.
  *Instructions:* Find a straight, 10-foot chip shot. Place one of the 2x4s about 16 inches ahead of the ball and in-line with where you want the ball to start — right at the edge of the fringe and green. Place the second 2x4 about 6 inches behind the ball at a slightly inward angle; this represents SweetSpot Path.

  As you make swings, pick the clubhead up immediately (not "low and slow") while keeping it directly on top of the rear 2x4 (Sweetspot Path). Avoid striking the rear 2x4 — if you strike it on the backswing, you didn't take the club back steeply enough, which can be due to moving your head back (disrupting the Steady Head), shifting your weight back, or not having enough Weight Forward. If you strike it on the downswing, you've disrupted the Flat Left Wrist.

  At follow-through, the clubface should be slightly closed in relation to the front 2x4 and your straight-line radius should be maintained. If either is incorrect, fix it so your hands know what the correct alignment feels like. Do this drill with and without a ball.

2x4 Drill at address.                    2x4 Drill at the top.

2x4 Drill at follow-through.

## Training Plan

As you train chipping (as well as all other types of swings), make sure that your focus is on performing the motion correctly, not on the ball. Don't let the ball's behavior negatively influence what you're working on.

Learn to properly execute the motion, even if you miss the ball at first — and then train until you don't miss it anymore. Also, remember to track your results each time you train chipping, as it's the only way to ensure you're continually making progress.

We recommend using the 2x4 Drill whenever you train chipping. Utilize the Clapping Drill whenever you have a few free minutes — you can do it anywhere.

**Train or Practice?**

Most golfers "practice." We prefer that you "train."

This is more than semantics; it's about shifting your mindset. Athletes train. Hobbyists practice.

Elite runners train for marathons. Olympic athletes train for their particular sports. As golf is an athletic endeavor, golfers should be "training" too.

You will chip 32 balls each from short and long distances for a total of 64 chips. You'll use each set of 32 balls in a very specific way.

First, chip four balls while using the 2x4s. As you chip these balls, consciously think about proper mechanics, and work to improve your clubface alignment and clubhead path.

Then, chip four balls without the 2x4s. For these four, remove from your head all swing thoughts and other noise. Just see the ball, see the hole, and chip the ball in the hole.

Repeat this (four chips with the 2x4s, four without) three more times for a total of 32 chips at that distance. Then, move on to the next distance and hit 32 chips in the same fashion.

Especially when working on long chips, experiment with varying your club selection. Gain a feel for how far the ball rolls after it lands when you use an 8 iron versus a sand wedge, for instance.

- **Short chips**
  *Distance:* 20 feet.
  *Objective:* Make the chip, with all missed chips stopping within 3 feet of the hole.

- **Long chips**
  *Distance:* 40 feet.
  *Objective:* Make the chip, with all missed chips stopping within 3 feet of the hole.

# Pitching

Your pitching motion will be built right on top of your chipping motion. In this chapter, we'll outline the basic pitching motion and teach you how to hit several specialty shots, including lob and bunker shots, which are based on a pitching motion.

Compared with a chipping motion, a pitching motion has two major differences. First, a pitch involves a longer backswing than a chip, but at its longest should go only to the point where your right forearm is parallel to the ground. Second, due to the longer length of the motion, your left wrist will be cocking during the backswing and uncocking during the downswing. Both of these differences provide more power.

Pitch shots are useful for a variety of circumstances on the course. They can be used for approach shots from 80 yards and in, as well as around the green when you're outside the range of a chip.

Some important concepts to keep in mind while pitching:

- **Remember the Keys and Educated Hands.** As with all swings, your pitching motion must be guided by your Educated Hands and comply with all 5 Simple Keys.

- **Clubface is (still) king.** As with chipping, it's imperative that you strike the ball with a square clubface. For standard pitch shots, we recommend using Clubface Motion A, though you can also use Clubface Motion B or C depending on your desired shot trajectory.

- **More carry, less roll.** Pitch shots generally carry most of the way to the hole and stop quickly once they land. Compared with a chip, a pitch normally has more air time and less ground time, though there are instances — such as when the pin is in the back of the green — when it's advantageous to have the ball roll more after landing.

- **Body motion is dictated by your hands.** A pitch, unlike a chip, will involve some body motion (specifically shoulder turn) because of the longer backswing. The proper amount of shoulder turn is whatever amount is necessary to enable your hands to reach the end of the backswing, and then to reach follow-through or finish.

- **For distance control, you've got options.** You can control the distance of your pitch shots in four different ways — shortening or lengthening your backswing (up to, but not beyond, the point where your right forearm is level to the ground); choking up or down on the grip; swinging your arms slower or faster; or changing clubs. Experiment to find out which method is easiest and most reliable for you.

- **Pitches are for control, not distance.** Don't try to squeeze every last yard out of a pitch shot. Choose the proper speed, length of swing, and club for a particular shot, and then make a smooth, controlled motion.

**Pre-shot**
Start by standing behind the ball. Remind yourself what you intend to do: Fly the ball most of the way to the hole and have it stop quickly after it lands.

As it did for chipping, your target line — an imaginary straight line that extends from the ball to the target — will serve as your guide while pitching. Select an intermediate target on your target line about 6 to 12 inches in front of the ball.

**Grip**
Your pitching grip will be exactly the same as what you learned for chipping. To take your pitching grip:

- Hold the club out in front of you and level to the ground. Place the club on the heel pad of your left hand and close your fingers around the grip.

Place the club on the heel pad of your left hand.

Close your fingers around the grip.

- Add your right hand to the club so that your left thumb fits between the grip and the "lifeline" of your right palm. Connect your right hand to your left hand using an overlapping, interlocking, or 10-finger (baseball) grip style.

Add your right hand to the club.

- Close your right hand around your left thumb and grip, ensuring that the first joint of your right hand index finger (your "trigger" finger) is on the back side of (not on top of or underneath) the grip so you can monitor sweetspot pressure which is critical for getting on Sweetspot Path.

Proper grip.

**Setup and Address**

- **Posture.** Begin by standing up straight with your feet shoulder-width apart. Place about 60 percent of your weight on your left foot. Then, bend forward from your hips and slightly flex your knees. Ensure your head is centered between your feet (unlike chipping, where your head was over your left foot).

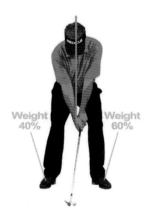

Proper posture.

- **Stance.** Your stance can be square or slightly open, though both feet should be slightly turned (flared) out.

Proper stance with feet slightly flared out.

Proper stance (down-the-line view).

- **Hands.** Place your hands so that the grip end of the club is pointing at the inside of your right thigh. The clubface will be square to the target and the clubshaft will be leaning slightly toward the target. Your left wrist will be bent and your right wrist will be flat - remember that at impact those will need to be reversed so you have a Flat Left Wrist.

Proper hand position.

- **Ball position.** The ball should be in the center of your chest.

Proper ball position.

**Making the Motion**
As always, strive to achieve all five Keys in every pitch you hit.

> **Startup and Backswing.** Just like with chipping, make a fanning motion with your right forearm to start the club back. Once your hands pass your right thigh, allow your right elbow to fold (bend) until your right forearm becomes parallel to the ground. Think "fan and fold" as you pick the club up with your right forearm.

While your hands are moving to the top your head is staying steady. The Steady Head is achieved by turning your shoulders perpendicular to your spine - your right shoulder must feel like it is going upward and backward while your left shoulder is going downward and inward. This creates a "stretching" of your right side and a "compressing" of your left side.

Startup and backswing.

Startup and backswing (down-the-line view).

- **Top.** At most, your right forearm is level to the ground. Your left arm has moved across your chest, while your left wrist has cocked due to your right arm bending and the momentum of your swing, not because you've deliberately cocked it. Check to ensure you're on plane — the grip end of the club should be pointing at the target line unless the clubshaft is parallel to the ground, in which case the clubshaft should be parallel to the target line. Your weight should have stayed on your left side.

Top.

Top (down-the-line view).

**Startdown and Downswing.** Turn your right shoulder toward the inside rear part of the ball, which in turn drives your hands toward the inside rear part of the ball. You'll feel sweetspot pressure intensify on the first joint of your right hand index finger which allows you to get on the Sweetspot Path. As your right shoulder turns, simultaneously allow your hips to slide toward the target (the bottom of your spine will move slightly forward — you don't tilt your head back), which will increase the amount of lower body weight on your left foot and begin creating Weight Forward. This slight hip slide also enables your right elbow to move in front of your right hip and your hands to travel in a straight line to Impact Hand Location. When your hands get in-line with your right thigh, your right forearm is pointing at your target line.

Downswing.

Downswing (down-the-line view).

- **Impact.** You've continued to turn your right shoulder toward the inside rear part of the ball and increase your Weight Forward. Your left forearm and Flat Left Wrist have turned into Impact Hand Location (your hands appear to you to be over the toes of your left foot, with the Flat Left Wrist facing the target). The clubface is now nearly square to the target, and you're on the Sweetspot Path because you've driven your accumulated sweetspot pressure into the inside rear part of the ball.

Impact.

- **Follow-through.** You've driven past impact, your left arm is being blasted off your chest, and both arms are straight. You have Clubface Control - since you're using Clubface Motion A, the clubface has continued to close and is now pointing about 70° to 80° across your target line (nearly parallel, but not quite). You take a divot, which begins after the ball is struck.

Follow-through.

Clubface Motion A.

Follow-through (down-the-line view).

- **Finish.** Your momentum has carried you past follow-through to a full finish, and you've maintained your balance. Nearly all of your weight, about 90 to 95 percent, is on your left foot. Your hands are near your left shoulder.

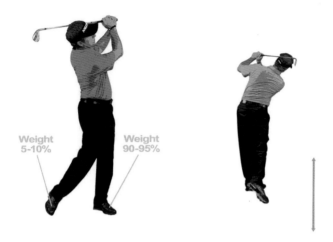

Weight
5-10%

Weight
90-95%

Finish.                                    Finish (down-the-line view).


**Drills**
These pitching drills — as with the chipping drills in the previous chapter — can be done at the course or at home, and with a ball or without a ball. The first one should even be done without a club.

- **Clapping Drill (for pitching)**
  *Purpose:* To educate your hands as to the feel of a proper pitching motion.
  *Equipment:* Just your hands.
  *Instructions:* Take an address position. Keeping your body, left arm, and left hand motionless, swing your right arm and hand back (fan) until you reach your right thigh, and then allow your right elbow to bend (fold) until your right forearm becomes parallel to the ground. Think "fan and fold" as you pick up your right forearm. Then, swing down until your right palm hits your left palm. Allow momentum to bring you to follow-through (both arms straight after impact).

Clapping Drill at address.          Clapping Drill at the top.

Clapping Drill at follow-though.

- **Line in the Sand Drill (for pitching)**
  *Purpose:* To educate your hands to maintain a Flat Left Wrist and
  sweetspot pressure during a pitching motion.
  *Equipment:* Sand wedge and a bunker.
  *Instructions:* In a bunker, take an address position and draw a line
  (perpendicular to your target line) just behind the center of your stance.
  Make a pitching motion, ensuring that you strike the sand in front of
  the line (to check, ensure your "sand divot" begins in front of the line).
  Stop at follow-through and make sure the clubshaft is leaning toward
  the target.

- **Great Wall of China Drill (for pitching)**

  *Purpose:* To educate your hands to maintain a Flat Left Wrist and sweetspot pressure during a pitching motion.

  *Equipment:* Sand wedge and a bunker.

  *Instructions:* In a bunker, build a wall of sand (perpendicular to your target line) approximately 6 inches high and 6 inches wide. Take an address position with the wall of sand in the center of your stance. Using a pitching motion, try to destroy the entire wall one swing at a time, ensuring you continue through the wall to follow-through. Focus on bringing the entire clubshaft, rather than just the clubhead, into impact. Check to make sure the clubshaft is leaning toward the target at follow-through.

**Training Plan**

Your training plan for pitching has two parts and differs slightly from the plans you have for chipping. Throughout part one, you'll be using one of the drills outlined above. For part two, you'll be hitting real shots from two different distances.

- **Part 1.** Choose one of the three pitching drills and set it up. (Ensure you rotate through these over time so you're not doing one much more often than the others.) Make four swings while consciously thinking about proper mechanics. Then, make four swings without conscious mechanical thoughts, letting your Educated Hands move the club as they know how. Repeat this (four with swing thoughts, four without) three more times for a total of 32 swings.

- **Part 2.** Find a pitch shot of about 20 yards, with at least 7 yards of space between the front edge of the green and the hole (use a towel as a target if necessary). Hit four pitch shots with a conscious focus on mechanics, and then four shots with no thoughts of mechanics. Repeat this three more times for a total of 32 pitch shots. Your objective is to get the ball within 6 feet of the hole.

  Then, find a pitch shot of about 30 yards, with at least 8 yards of space between the front edge of the green and the hole/target. Hit 32 pitch shots in the same manner as before. Your objective is to get the ball within 9 feet of the hole.

**Quick Tips: Pitching**

- Weight slightly favors your left foot at address and throughout the swing
- Ball is positioned in-line with your sternum
- Think "fan and fold" as you pick up your right forearm in the backswing
- Right forearm does not exceed parallel to the ground in the backswing
- Left wrist will cock in the backswing, but you don't deliberately cock it

As with chipping training, remember to track your results for part two of the pitching training plan — write down how many of your shots stopped within 6 feet (from 20 yards) and 9 feet (from 30 yards). This kind of tracking is the only way to ensure that you're continually making progress.

**Specialty Pitch Shots**
With only minimal changes, your pitching motion can be used to tackle several common specialty shots. You'll see that the biggest changes are during setup and address, with the actual motion staying relatively constant. You still must comply with the four Keys.

- **Standard Bunker Shots.** As you may know, your goal in a bunker is not to actually hit the ball — it's to strike the sand behind the ball and allow the sand to "throw" the ball onto the green. Unless the ball is buried, you also don't want the club to dig into the sand; you want it to glide or splash through the sand.

  To get the club to glide through the sand, you first have to expose the bounce (the trailing edge) of the clubhead. You do this by opening the clubface — turning it slightly to your right — before taking your grip. From there, set your body and stance slightly open (aimed left), which will compensate for your open clubface. Set your ball position as you would for a standard pitch shot. Put slightly more weight on your left foot and keep it there during the swing.

  As with all pitch shots, try to keep your body as quiet as possible as you make the swing, which will be steeper – more up and down – than for a normal pitch shot. Your arms and club will move more like the letter "V" with the feeling of picking the club up quickly rather than the letter "U" of a full swing. Swing the club along your slightly open stance line and try to aggressively enter the sand a couple inches behind the ball. You'll use Clubface Motion C, so at follow-through the clubface should be perpendicular to your target line and facing the sky.

- **Buried Bunker Shots.** With a buried bunker shot, you need to drive — rather than splash — the ball onto the green. You'll use Clubface Motion B. Set up with the clubface slightly closed, while also setting your body and stance slightly closed (aimed right). Put most of your weight on your left foot. As you make your swing, try to feel as if you're digging the clubhead into the bunker. Be aggressive.

- **Lob Shots.** A lob shot is very much like a bunker shot, except that it's done from the grass or a very firm grassless surface (hardpan). For lob shots you'll use a lob wedge instead of a sand wedge, as the higher loft of the lob wedge will result in a higher trajectory and softer landing.

  Set up your body and ball position as you would for any other pitch shot. You have the option of a square or open stance — whichever you choose, ensure you swing the club along your stance line.

The key to the lob shot is to not allow the clubface to turn over (close) during impact or follow-through. This is why you'll use Clubface Motion C, where the clubface will be facing the sky through impact and at follow-through.

- **Uneven Lies.** The objective with uneven lies is to make them even lies, which requires only some slight modifications to your address position. After this you'll simply make a normal pitching motion.

  If the ball is on a downhill or uphill lie, align your shoulders with the slope to make it an even lie.

  If the ball is above or below your feet, adjust the clubhead at address so that the sole sits flat on the slope, making sure that neither the toe nor the heel of the club is in the air. To achieve this, you will likely have to place your hands a little lower on the grip (closer to where the grip ends and the metal of the shaft begins) when the ball is above your feet, or higher on the grip (closer to the end of the club) when the ball is below your feet.

  Use these same processes for dealing with uneven lies for shots requiring full swings.

## Full Swing

Everything we've done to this point has been designed to make you a better player while helping you understand the mechanical aspects of your golf swing. We've outlined the concept of Educated Hands; the role of the body, arms, and hands in the golf swing; and the 5 Simple Keys that must be achieved during every swing.

We then started the process of building your swing from the ground up. We started with chipping, where we began educating your hands and teaching you how to produce — and reproduce the 5 Simple Keys. We then moved on to pitching, which is essentially an extended chipping motion.

Now, we'll increase the length of your motion once again — adding more body motion along the way — to create the "total motion" of the full swing.

Some important concepts to keep in mind for the full swing:

- **Remember the Keys and Educated Hands.** As with all swings, your full swing motion must be guided by your Educated Hands and comply with all 5 Simple Keys.

- **The full swing is built on all that's come before it.** Don't intimidate yourself by thinking the full swing is entirely different than any other golf motion — it's not. If your chipping and pitching motions are solid, you should have just a short learning curve as you begin utilizing your Educated Hands and the 5 Simple Keys in the full swing.

- **Pitching motions are nearly full swings.** If you make a pitching motion and then swing your hands back another foot or so, you've made a full swing. There's a slight bit more to it than that, but not much. If you can properly execute the pitching motion, you've got 80 percent of the full swing in the bag.

- **As the motion lengthens, errors are magnified.** Errors in the full swing are always due to errors in shorter swings. Problems that seemed small while chipping quickly become glaring faults during full swings. If during the full swing you feel like your hands are not fully educated and the Keys are imprecise, go back and focus on chips and pitches.

- **Clubface is (still) king.** As with chipping and pitching, it's critical that you strike the ball with a square clubface. For standard full swings, we recommend using Clubface Motion A, though you can also use Clubface Motion B depending on your desired shot trajectory.

- **Your hands move in a straight line.** The shortest and easiest way to connect two points is to draw a straight line. For that reason, we prefer that you move your hands in a straight line from address to the top to Impact Hand Location.

**Pre-shot**
Start by standing behind the ball. Establish your target line and then select an intermediate target on that line about 2 to 3 feet in front of the ball. The intermediate target you choose should be visible out of your peripheral vision once you take your address position.

**Grip**
Your full swing grip is identical to your pitching grip. As a refresher, here's the process:

- Hold the club out in front of you and level to the ground. Place the club on the heel pad of your left hand and close your fingers around the grip.

Place the club on the heel pad of your left hand.

**What about grip pressure?**

Opinions vary as far as the "proper" grip pressure for full swings, but you'll most often hear instructors suggest gentle, light grip pressures (on a 1-10 scale, a 3 or 4).

In contrast, we recommend a firm grip pressure (on a 1-10 scale, an 8).

Your hands should act as clamps on the golf club. Remember that the ball strikes the clubface with the same force that the face strikes the ball.

If your grip pressure is too light, your hands will tend to wobble or change position during the swing and under the stress of impact.

Close your fingers around the grip.

- Add your right hand to the club so that your left thumb fits between the grip and the "lifeline" of your right palm. Connect your right hand to your left hand using an overlapping, interlocking, or 10-finger (baseball) grip style.

Add your right hand to the club.

- Close your right hand around your left thumb and grip, ensuring that the first joint of your right hand index finger (your "trigger" finger) is on the back side of (not on top of or underneath) the grip so you can monitor sweetspot pressure, which is critical for getting on the Sweetspot Path.

Proper grip.

## Setup and Address

As we mentioned in the chipping chapter, it takes no athletic ability at all to set up properly to a golf ball. A full-length mirror, such as the kind you might have in your closet, is a wonderful tool for ensuring your stance, posture, and hand and ball position are as good as they can be.

- **Posture.** Begin by standing up straight with your feet shoulder-width apart and your weight evenly distributed — half on your right side, half on your left side. Then, bend forward from your hips, slightly flex your knees, and ensure your head is centered between your feet.

Proper posture.

- **Stance.** Your stance should be square, with both feet slightly turned (flared) out.

Proper stance.

Proper stance
(down-the-line view).

- **Hands.** Place your hands ether in the center of your body ( in-line with your belt buckle) or slightly forward (with the grip end of the club pointing at the inside of your left thigh). The clubface will be square to the target; the clubshaft will be perpendicular to the ground or leaning slightly forward. Your left wrist will be bent and your right wrist will be flat - remember that by impact those will need to be reversed so you have a Flat Left Wrist.

Proper hand position.

- **Ball Position.** Ball position will vary in the full swing depending on the club you're using. When you consider ball position, think in relation to your upper body and not in relation to your feet. The width of your stance changes during the course of a round, but the width of your upper body does not. As a starting point, use these guidelines: ball in the center of your chest for a wedge; ball in-line with the logo on your shirt for a 5 iron; ball in-line with your armpit for a driver. We emphasize that these are starting points — you'll have to experiment on your own to refine them — because the intricacies of your individual swing will influence the ball positions you'll need to use to hit straight shots.

Ball position varies based on the club you're using.

## Making the Motion
As with all shots, strive to achieve all five Keys in every full swing. Once your hands are properly trained, making the full swing is literally as simple as allowing your Educated Hands to start at address and move to shoulder height (top), then Impact Hand Location, and finally to the finish.

- **Startup and Backswing.** Just as with chipping and pitching, make a fanning motion with your right forearm to start the club back. Once your hands pass your right thigh, allow your right elbow to fold (bend) until your hands reach shoulder height. This entire motion will feel as though you're "raising your right hand" to be sworn in to testify in court. Check to ensure you're on plane — the clubhead or grip end of the club should be pointing at your target line unless the clubshaft is parallel to the ground, in which case the clubshaft should be parallel to your target line.

While your hands are moving to the top your head is staying steady. The Steady Head is achieved by turning your shoulders perpendicular to your spine – your right shoulder must feel like it is going upward and backward while the left shoulder is going downward and inward. This creates a "stretching" of your right side and a "compressing" of your left side.

Startup.

Startup (down-the-line view).

Backswing.

Backswing (down-the-line view).

- **Top.** Your hands are at shoulder height, with your left arm having moved across your chest. Your shoulders and hips have turned sharply around your spine, but only enough to accommodate your hand position. Your left wrist has cocked, not because you've deliberately cocked it but due to the momentum of your swing. The clubface, since you're using Clubface Motion A, has opened in relation to the target line (though you haven't consciously opened it). Your head is still in the center of your feet meaning you've maintained a Steady Head. You can check to ensure you're on plane by looking at the grip end of the club - it should be pointing at the target line.

Top.                                    Top (down-the-line view).

- **Startdown.** As you did for pitching, turn your right shoulder toward the inside rear part of the ball, which in turn drives your hands toward the inside rear part of the ball. As your right shoulder turns, simultaneously allow your hips to slide toward the target (the bottom of your spine will move slightly forward — you don't tilt your head back), which will increase the amount of lower body weight on your left foot and begin creating Weight Forward. This slight hip slide also enables your right elbow to move in front of your right hip and your hands to travel in a straight line to Impact Hand Location.

Startdown.                                    Startdown (down-the-line view).

- **Downswing.** Continue moving your right shoulder and hands toward the inside rear portion of the ball and increasing your Weight Forward. You'll feel sweetspot pressure continue to intensify on the first joint of your right hand index finger putting you on the Sweetspot Path. You're aware of the need to get your hands to Impact Hand Location, and you let your Educated Hands find that spot.

Downswing.                                    Downswing (down-the-line view).

- **Release Point.** Your hands are in-line with your right thigh. Your right forearm is pointing at, and the clubshaft is parallel to, your target line. Your right shoulder and hands are continuing to move toward the inside rear portion of the ball while sweetspot pressure is being steadily maintained on the first joint of your right hand index finger keeping you on the Sweetspot Path.

Release point.                Release point
                              (down-the-line view).

- **Impact.** Your left forearm and Flat Left Wrist have turned into Impact Hand Location (your hands appear to you to be over the toes of your left foot, with the Flat Left Wrist facing the target). Your left arm and the clubshaft form a straight line (representing the radius of the swing). You've maintained a Steady Head, and you have your Weight Forward. The clubface is now nearly square to the target, and you're on the Sweetspot Path because you've driven your accumulated Sweetspot Pressure into the inside rear part of the ball as if you're trying to drive the ball into the ground.

Impact.

- **Follow-through.** You've driven past impact, your left arm is being blasted off your chest, and both arms are straight. You have Clubface Control – since you're using Clubface Motion A, the clubface has continued to close and is now pointing about 70° to 80° across your target line (nearly parallel, but not quite). For all clubs except the driver, you've taken a divot after striking the ball.

Follow-through.                    Clubface Motion A

Follow-through
(down-the-line view).

- **Finish.** Your momentum has carried you past follow-through. Your hands are over your left shoulder, the clubshaft is crossing behind your head, both arms are folded (bent), nearly all of your weight (90 to 95 percent), is on your left foot and you've maintained your balance.

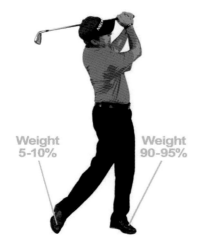

Weight
5-10%

Weight
90-95%

Finish.

Finish (down-the-line view).

**Drills**

The drills we prescribe for the full swing are simply extended versions of two drills you've seen before. These both can be done without a club, meaning you can do them just about anywhere — at home, at the office, or at the course (they make a great pre-round warm-up for your Educated Hands).

- **Clapping Drill (for full swing)**

  *Purpose:* To educate your hands as to the feel of a proper full swing motion.

  *Equipment:* Just your hands.

  *Instructions:* Take an address position. Keeping your body, left arm, and left hand motionless, swing your right arm and hand back (fan) until you reach your right thigh, and then allow your right elbow to bend (fold) until your hands reach shoulder height.

  This entire motion will feel as though you're "raising your right hand" to be sworn in to testify in court. Then, swing down until your right palm hits your left palm. Allow momentum to bring you to follow-through (both arms straight after impact) and finish (hands over your left shoulder).

Clapping Drill at address.

Clapping Drill at the top.

Clapping Drill at follow-through.

- **Line in the Sand Drill (for full swing)**
  *Purpose:* To educate your hands to maintain a Flat Left Wrist and sweetspot pressure during a full swing.
  *Equipment:* Sand wedge and a bunker.
  *Instructions:* In a bunker, take an address position and draw a line (perpendicular to your target line) just behind the center of your stance. Make a full swing, ensuring that you strike the sand in front of the line (to check, ensure your "sand divot" begins in front of the line). Stop at follow-through and make sure the clubshaft is leaning toward the target.

- **Great Wall of China Drill (for full swing)**
  *Purpose:* To educate your hands to maintain a Flat Left Wrist and sweetspot pressure during a full swing.
  *Equipment:* Sand wedge and a bunker.
  *Instructions:* In a bunker, build a wall of sand (perpendicular to your target line) approximately 6 inches high and 6 inches wide. Take an address position with the wall of sand in the center of your stance. Using a full swing, try to destroy the entire wall one swing at a time, ensuring you continue through the wall to follow-through. Focus on bringing the entire clubshaft, rather than just the clubhead, into impact. Check to make sure the clubshaft is leaning toward the target at follow-through.

**Training Plan**
The training plan for the full swing includes the same 32-ball technique you've seen in the training plans for chipping and pitching.

The full swing should be trained in groups of 32 shots, with each group dedicated to improving only one of the Keys. Trying to fix everything at once will actually hinder your progress, so work to incrementally improve each Key one at a time — and watch as your game improves.

Within each group of 32 balls, you'll hit eight shots each with four different clubs: a wedge (sand or pitching wedge), a short iron (8 or 9 iron), a middle iron (6 or 7 iron), and your driver.

After choosing the Key you'll be focusing on for this 32-ball batch, start with your wedge and hit four shots while consciously focusing on executing the proper mechanics for that Key. Then, hit four shots where you remove all swing thoughts and other mental noise.

Switch to your next club (a short iron) and repeat the process: four shots while focused on mechanics, four shots while not. Repeat again with your middle iron and driver for a total of 32 shots. Consider this one "unit" of training.

If you wish to hit more than 32 balls in a training session, go ahead — just select another Key and work through the above process with another batch of 32 balls.

**Variable and Invariable Shot Training**
There are two types of training (practice):

- **Invariable Shot Training,** is when you work on developing a specific skill or motion by hitting the same type of shot many times in a row with the same club. This should sound familiar, as it's essentially what we prescribe in our training plans in this book.

- **Variable Shot Training,** is when you hit a variety of shots without hitting the same shot twice in a row, similar to what you have to do on the golf course.

**Quick Tips: Full swing**

- In pre-shot, precisely program the type of shot you want to hit
- Trust your motion, and let your motion make the shot
- Maintain a smooth rhythm, ensuring your left arm and the clubshaft are in-line from impact to follow-through
- Swing at a pace where you can effectively control the clubshaft, clubhead, and clubface

During your full swing training sessions, begin by following the training plan outlined above. Afterward, spend some time on variable shot training — while still on the practice tee, envision a golf course that you know well and literally hit shots as if you were playing there.

For example, if the first hole on the course you choose is a short par 4, you'd hit one shot with a driver followed by one with a 9 iron. Then, go on to the next hole and "play" it, continuing on through all 18 holes. To make this training even more realistic, do your best to find different lies and conditions on the practice tee, and add some pressure by competing with your friends.

Regularly using variable shot training has several advantages. First, it forces you to get outside your comfort zone — away from the perfect fairway lies of the practice tee — and contend with a wide variety of lies and shots, which prepares you for when you encounter them on the course.

Also, until properly trained, your brain does not know the difference between good and bad motions, or why a certain motion produces a certain type of ball flight. When you try to hit a variety of shots — high, low, draws, fades — and practice applying different Clubface Motions, you're training your brain and hands to feel the subtle changes you need to make in your swing to produce each type of shot.

Finally, variable shot training improves your ability to hit straight shots — the most difficult shots in golf — because learning to hit different types of shots tightens your shot dispersion.

Variable shot training challenges you to experiment, execute, and learn. We strongly encourage you to incorporate variable shot training into your overall practice routine — for every minute of invariable shot training, try to perform two minutes of variable shot training.

# Mastering Ball Flight

Understanding ball flight is critical if you want to be able to self-diagnose your golf swing. Without some working knowledge of ball flight laws and how to manipulate your ball flight, you're left guessing as to why a particular shot flew as it did.

You may have to review this chapter a few times before things "click." Be patient, experiment, and soon enough you'll be on your way to understanding the different types of ball flights (shot shapes) and mastering ball flight control.

When you become an expert at ball flight control, you'll benefit in two ways.

First, intentional draws and fades can open the door to lower scores. While high handicappers are happy to simply get the ball on the green, low handicappers are shooting at pins in an effort to make birdies.

Getting the ball close to the pin often requires shaping the shot — a pin tucked in the front right part of the green calls for a high fade, for instance. The same concept holds true on tee shots, as being able to place the ball on a specific side of the fairway is important if you're going to attack the flag. Draws and fades can also be used to mitigate crosswinds on tee shots and approach shots.

Second, you'll learn to hit the ball straighter. Yes, you read that correctly. By teaching your brain the differences in how your swing feels when you hit a straight shot versus a draw versus a fade, your normal swing — which should produce a rather straight shot — will become more consistent and effective.

## Ball Flight Laws

The golf ball stays in contact with the clubface for only a few ten-thousandths of a second. It's during this very short impact interval when the ball receives its flight plan for that particular shot — how far to go, at what trajectory, and with what curvature (if any).

The two most important factors that influence ball flight are:

- **Clubface Direction.** Depending on the club being used, clubface direction — where the clubface is pointing — when the ball leaves the clubface is responsible for upward of 85 percent of the ball's initial direction. The clubhead path is only minimally responsible for the ball's initial direction. Essentially, the ball will start in the direction the clubface is pointing when the ball leaves the clubface.

  The takeaway point from this is clear: If your shot began to the right of your target, the clubface was open in relation to your target (pointing to the right of it) when the ball left the clubface, and vice versa if your shot began to the left of your target.

- **Clubhead Path.** Shots that curve — draws, fades, hooks, and slices — result from a difference (divergence) between where the clubface is pointing and the direction of the clubhead path when the ball leaves the clubface. Shots that have no curvature — shots straight at the target, straight pushes, and straight pulls — are a result of a perfect match between the clubface direction and clubhead path.

  If the clubface is open in relation to the clubhead path (clubface is pointing to the right of the direction the clubhead is moving), the ball will curve from left to right. Likewise, if the clubface is closed in relation to the clubhead path, the ball will curve from right to left.

  Curvature is a matter of degree — literally. More curvature is a result of a greater divergence (measured in degrees) between the clubface direction and clubhead path. For example, a giant slice is due to a clubface that's severely open to the clubhead path.

When self-diagnosing your ball flight, focus mainly on clubface direction and clubhead path, but recognize that several other factors — including impact quality (whether or not you struck the ball on the clubface's sweetspot), clubhead speed, and weather — can also influence ball curvature.

**Types of Ball Flight**
The causes of nine common ball flights are outlined in this table. While you will be used to thinking about the clubface in relation to the target, note that we talk about the clubhead path in relation to the clubface — not the target. For ball flight purposes, it's irrelevant whether the clubhead path

is moving straight at, or right or left of, the target. All that matters is the direction it's moving when compared with where the clubface is pointing.

| # | Ball Flight | Clubface ( in relation to target) | Clubhead Path (in relation to clubface) |
|---|---|---|---|
| 1 | Starts straight, no curve (truly straight) | Square | Square |
| 2 | Starts straight, curves left (hook) | Square | Moving to the right |
| 3 | Starts straight, curves right (slice) | Square | Moving to the left |
| 4 | Starts right, no curve (straight push) | Open | Square |
| 5 | Starts right, curves left (draw) | Open | Moving to the right |
| 6 | Starts right, curves right (push slice) | Open | Moving to the left |
| 7 | Starts left, no curve (straight pull) | Closed | Square |
| 8 | Starts left, curves right (fade) | Closed | Moving to the left |
| 9 | Starts left, curves left (pull hook) | Closed | Moving to the right |

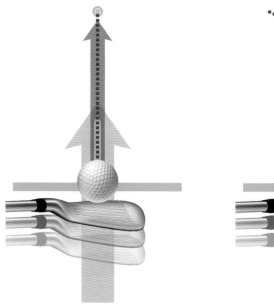

1. Truly Straight.

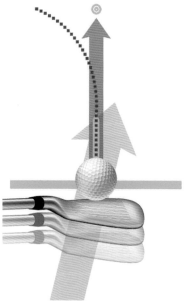

2. Hook.

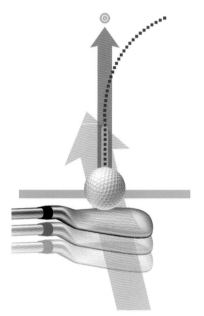

3. Slice.

4. Straight Push.

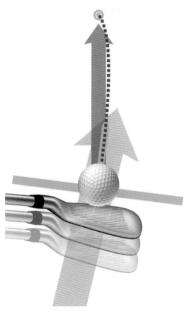

5. Draw.

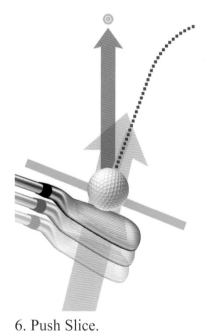

6. Push Slice.

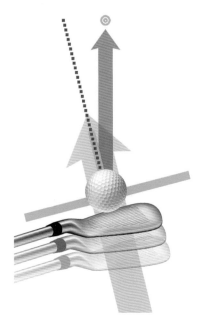

7. Straight Pull.

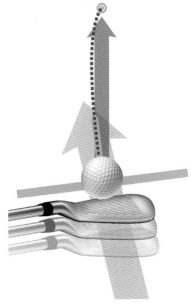

8. Fade.

9. Pull Hook.

In terms of degrees, very minor changes have a huge impact on ball flight. If you look at a clock, the very small distance between 12:00 and 12:01 is 6°. In golf, a variance of 6° is more than enough to send the ball way off target, as this image shows.

The red dots at the top represent the face of a clock, with each dot representing one minute before or after 12:00. With the clubface pointed just one minute (6°) to the left or right of 12:00 — and with the clubhead path matching that clubface direction — a 100-yard shot would miss the target by 31 feet while a 250-yard shot would miss by 26 yards. These numbers stay constant regardless of the club being used.

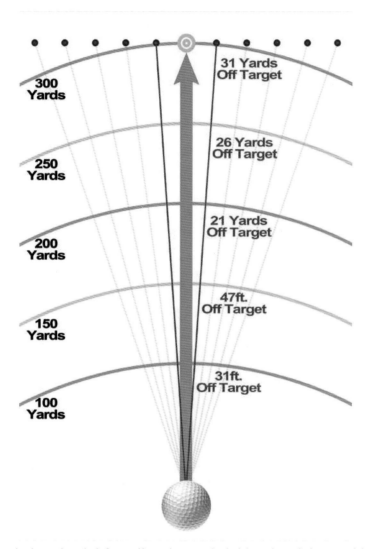

Minor variations in clubface direction and clubhead path have a big impact on ball flight.

Let's look at some examples using degree figures:

- **Slice (image #3).** One shot that higher handicappers are used to hitting is a slice, which is when the ball starts toward the target but then curves severely to the right. For the ball to start straight, the clubface must be square to the target — 0° open or closed — when the ball leaves it. The severe left-to-right ball flight is due to the clubhead path moving 3° to the left of where the clubface is pointing.

- **Draw (image #5).** For a basic draw, the clubface might be 1° open to the target when the ball leaves the clubface, causing the shot to start to the right of the target. For the ball to curve to the left and land at the target, the clubhead path would be moving 0.5° to the right of where the clubface is pointing.

- **Pull Hook (image #9).** For better players, erratic shots are more often hooks than slices. A pull hook, which is when the ball starts to the left of the target and curves further left, is one type of hook. With this shot, the clubface is pointing 1° to the left of the target when the ball leaves it. The right-to-left curvature is a result of the clubhead path moving 1.5° to the right of where the clubface is pointing.

Note that these are just examples and that other combinations of clubface direction and clubhead path can produce slices, draws, and pull hooks. For example, a clubface that is 2° open to the target with a clubhead path moving 1° to the right of the clubface will also produce a draw, and it'll be a larger draw than in the example above.

**Manipulating Ball Flight**

Now that you know what governs initial direction and curvature — clubface direction and clubhead path, and the relationship between the two when the ball leaves the clubface — let's outline how you can intentionally shape your shots. Intentional curvature, however, should be used sparingly. Straight shots maximize distance and accuracy, so strive to hit the ball straight whenever possible.

Ensure you "program in" any intended curvature during the pre-shot process and rehearse your motion appropriately. Then, let the motion make the shot.

- **Draw (starts right, curves left, and lands at your target)**
  Aim your entire body and the clubface square to your target (a normal setup). As you make your motion, intentionally swing slightly out to the right, which creates a slightly open clubhead path. Keep the clubface slightly open to your target, but closed to your clubhead path.

- **Fade (starts left, curves right, and lands at your target)**
  Aim your entire body and the clubface square to your target (a normal setup). As you make your motion, intentionally swing in to the left, which creates a slightly open clubhead path. Keep the clubface slightly closed to your target, but open to your clubhead path.

## Drill
To learn how to manipulate your ball flight, you need only this one comprehensive drill.

- **Shot Shaping Drill**
  *Purpose:* To educate your hands to produce straight shots, draws, and fades on command.
  *Equipment:* A club, five 42-inch sticks or dowels, a ruler, and golf balls.
  *Instructions:* Set up the five sticks or dowels as shown in the image. The orange line (two sticks) represents the target line, the green lines (two sticks) represent the clubhead path after impact, and the red line (one stick) represents the Sweetspot Path.

  There should be just less than 4.5 inches of distance from the tips (far left in image) of the clubhead path sticks to the target line stick, and just more than 8 inches of distance from the tip (far right in image) of the Sweetspot Path stick to the target line stick.

  Practice hitting different shot shapes — straight shots, draws, and fades — by moving your clubhead path over each stick with the correct clubface direction for your intended shot shape.

  To hit a straight shot, direct your clubhead path over the center stick with a clubface that's square to the target when the ball leaves it.

  To hit a draw, direct your clubhead path over the outside (top) stick with a clubface that's slightly open to the target when the ball leaves it.

To hit a fade, direct your clubhead path over the inside (bottom) stick with a clubface that's slightly closed to the target when the ball leaves it.

If your shot shape is not what you intend — for example, if you're trying to hit a draw but hit a straight push instead — go back and review the early sections of this chapter. It has all the information you need to diagnose what's going wrong.

## 42" Alignment Sticks

## 4 ⁷⁄₁₆" Separations                    8 ¹⁄₁₆" Separation

Proper setup of Shot Shaping Drill.

**Training Plan**
Your training plan for ball flight control has two parts. In part one, you'll be using the Shot Shaping Drill. In part two, you'll be hitting a variety of shots to simulate on-course play.

- **Part 1.** You'll make 96 swings — 48 without a ball but while guided by the drill, and 48 with a ball but without the aid of the drill.

  To begin, without balls but guided by the drill, make four swings over the center stick. Then, with balls but without the aid of the drill, hit four straight shots. Repeat this three more times for a total of 32 swings, 16 of which were real shots.

  Next, pick a different club. Without balls but guided by the drill, make four swings over the outside (top) stick. Then, with balls but without the aid of the drill, hit four draws. Repeat this three more times for a total of 32 swings, 16 of which were real shots.

Pick a different club again. Without balls but guided by the drill, make four swings over the inside (bottom) stick, and then hit four fades without the aid of the drill. Repeat this three more times for a total of 32 swings, 16 of which were real shots.

You've now made 96 total swings, 48 of which were real shots. After each real shot, take note of where the ball starts and how it curves (if at all). Begin to notice the subtle differences in how your swing feels when you hit a straight shot versus a draw versus a fade.

- **Part 2.** Once you finish your 96 swings, use variable shot training to play an imaginary 18 holes of golf on the practice tee. As explained earlier in the book, variable shot training involves envisioning a golf course you know well and hitting shots, as if you were playing a round there.

# Taking it to the Course

The majority of golfers — PGA Tour professionals included — hit much better shots on the practice tee than they do on the course.

This brings us to one of the most perplexing questions in golf: "Why can't I take it from the practice tee to the course?"

It's common to see golfers who are the equivalent of single-digit handicappers on the practice tee but 30-handicappers on the course. They can stand on the practice tee and hit even the smallest targets while working the ball left, right, high, or low. They have the hands of a surgeon, and have the golf club and golf ball under their complete control. Yet, they lose it all when they step up to the first tee.

The solution is to learn to separate training from playing.

- **Training.** A time for observation and adjustment where you focus on individual mechanical components of your swing. Shot direction and outcome should often be immaterial.

- **Playing.** A time for concentration, discipline, and execution where you focus on making a fully unified, smooth motion. Shot direction and outcome are of the utmost importance.

The bridge that takes you from the practice tee to the golf course is variable shot training, which we introduced earlier. At some point during your training sessions, you have to hit shots as if you were playing a round of golf.

When you step to the first tee, you must be able to eliminate all mechanical thoughts and simply see the ball, see the target, and hit the ball to the target. Let your motion make the shot.

### Pre-shot Process
Since every shot you hit is different in one way or another, each one of them must be individually programmed into your computer (also known as your brain). This happens during the "pre-shot process" — we don't call it a "pre-shot routine" because no two shots are alike.

The emphasis during the pre-shot process is on the motion you intend to make, not on striking the ball. This motion, in turn, will produce the desired shot.

The pre-shot process has three components:

- **Shot Assessment.** Choosing the appropriate shot type and club based on an evaluation of the lie, weather, course conditions, design of the hole, pin placement, and how you're feeling that day.

- **Shot Rehearsal.** Standing behind the ball and "programming in" the motion necessary to produce the intended shot type. If it's a standard chip, pitch, or full swing, rehearse the appropriate motion and visualize how the ball will fly. If it's a specialty shot, rehearse the motion that will produce that shot and visualize how the ball will fly.

- **Shot Setup.** Approaching the ball and taking your address position based on the programming you've already completed. From here, you simply execute the motion you programmed in. Most poorly executed shots are "missed" at address because players make last-minute changes to what they intend to do. By the time you're over the ball, you must fully trust your programming — if you don't, step away from the ball and restart the pre-shot process.

## Going on Automatic

Eliminating swing thoughts is your biggest challenge during a round of golf.

Now, we're not saying that you shouldn't think about each and every shot — you should. However, all of this should be done during the pre-shot process, not during the actual swing.

Eliminating swing thoughts means playing on "automatic." This means that during your swing, your mind is somewhere else — thinking about anything but your golf swing. When on "automatic," you're relying on built-in habits, not on conscious manipulation of your swing.

The majority of players today play on "manual." Even after an extensive pre-shot process, they set up over the ball with their minds still racing. During the swing, they are thinking mechanically and going over in their heads the myriad steps they must take during the backswing and downswing.

So just how do you eliminate swing thoughts? Essentially, all you have to do is deliberately keep your mind occupied with something else, such as a phrase or song ("Mary had a little lamb, I wish I had one too"). The only requirement is that it must not contain any action words. Your objective is to repeat this in your mind — methodically, rhythmically, and at a constant pace — beginning from the moment you start to address the ball and continuing until you reach the finish.

Playing on "automatic" doesn't guarantee that you'll hit great shots; it only guarantees that your ingrained habits shine through. If your habits are poor, you'll get poor results — and vice versa.

As you play on "automatic," pay close attention to trends in shot quality and ball flight, and use this information to identify areas for improvement. Go back and review the 5 Simple Keys, and structure your training sessions such that you spend the most time working to improve the Key(s) you suspect are responsible for your erroneous shots.

**Continual Learning**
From your best shots to your worst shots, you'll learn something from each one. Regardless of how you play on a given day, your computer (brain) is gathering and processing data at a speed you cannot comprehend. This data is archived and accessed to help you make on-course decisions in the future.

This is why an unusual shot — for example, having to intentionally hit a big hook around a tree — is difficult the first time you encounter it. You have no experiences (data) to rely on. The second and third times you encounter that type of shot, it's easier and you're more comfortable because you have mental data on what swing motion and shot type worked (or didn't work) before.

# Final Thoughts

Now that you've finished reading the *Medicus® PureStrike™ Golf Swing*, we trust that you're looking forward to your next visit to the practice tee. In creating this book, our goal was to provide you with science-based information in an easy-to-understand manner, along with clear training plans to help you systematically improve.

When you picked up this book, you may have been frustrated or discouraged with the state of your golf game — or even ready to stash your clubs in the basement for good. We hope we've re-energized your outlook on the game by showing you that there really is a better way to approach the golf swing.

We've explained in the simplest way possible how the golf swing works and what truly matters — Educated Hands and the 5 Simple Keys. And we've given you training plans for chipping, pitching, and the full swing that will help you break your old, incorrect habits.

In the preceding chapters, it was our job — as the instructor — to inform and explain. Now, it's your turn — as the student — to absorb and apply. Yes, this all requires some training to master, and there are no quick fixes. But at the same time, isn't it refreshing to know that golf doesn't have to be impossibly complex?

**The Medicus PureStrike™ Golf Swing in Three Lessons**
Most everything we've emphasized can be summarized into three concepts:

- **Educated Hands.** Your hands are educated when they've been trained to produce the five keys, arrive at Impact Hand Location, and know the precise route they must take from address to the top to impact to the finish.

- **The 5 Simple Keys.** To improve your golf swing's consistency, power, and precision, you must diligently work to continually improve how well you execute the 5 Simple Keys.

- **Building Your Swing - from the ground up.** Chipping, pitching, and the full swing build right on top of one another like layers, and errors in longer swings are due to errors in shorter ones.

**Perfect Training**

As we stated in this book's introduction, we strongly believe that anyone can achieve a single-digit handicap if five to 10 hours a week are devoted to golf learning and training. Though several of these five to 10 hours can be spent learning (such as reviewing this book and making notes), the rest must be dedicated to physical training — drills at home or at the course, slow-motion swings in front of a mirror, and time in the short game area and on the practice tee.

The old saying goes, "Practice (training) makes perfect." Actually, training makes permanent, which explains why many golfers can train endlessly, yet only have strongly ingrained poor habits to show for it.

For training to make perfect, you have to be training perfectly. This means using the training plans we've provided for chipping, pitching, and the full swing. It also means being deliberate, patient, and even slow during your training sessions.

Work to improve just one piece of your swing at a time. Visualize each shot you intend to hit. Look at and examine your alignments during slow-motion swings. If you're working through this book with a friend, have him or her watch you swing and verify that you're actually making the motion that you think you're making. Pay attention to your ball flight to see how it changes when you make a proper versus improper swing, and put that information into your mental database so it can be used later to self-diagnose swing problems. Utilize training aids (more on this in a moment). After training sessions, make notes about anything you discovered.

There are no shortcuts. Learning to make a better golf swing is no different than learning any other physical skill, be it playing a musical instrument or performing surgery. Regular training over time is the only path to mastery.

**Managing Expectations for Improvement**

Though the *Medicus® PureStrike™ Golf Swing* has given you the proper information you need to build and refine your golf swing, make no mistake — the golf swing habits you have today are deeply ingrained. If you've played golf for years or decades, just think about how many swings you've made — both on the course and practice tee — with each one reinforcing your bad habits just a little bit more.

On the upside, our experience has shown us that it doesn't take long at all for students to comprehend what they're doing wrong and demonstrate proper technique in slow-motion swings. But old habits come back quickly once students starting swinging at normal speed or head out on the course. In fact, old habits never really go away — you just overwrite the bad habit with a new, better habit, and must then ensure that the new habit is executed on the course.

It's normal to have progress come in bursts, followed by a plateau. At times, you may even regress slightly. This is no cause for alarm, especially when you consider that it's not uncommon for PGA Tour professionals to perform well in a tournament one week and perform poorly the very next week.

**Monitoring Your Improvement**
In golf, feel isn't always real. You can feel as though you're making a proper motion, but that's no guarantee you're actually making a proper motion — especially when you're trying to build new habits. Golfers have very little ability to monitor what they're doing during training, as they have no metrics or objective indicators of progress.

PGA Tour professionals overcome this obstacle by utilizing training aids, which offer the metrics and feedback necessary for them to continually monitor and track all aspects of their swings. These products also promote proper alignment, rhythm, plane, and more.

Training aids can significantly reduce your level of frustration by being a reliable "second set of eyes," instantly confirming whether or not you're properly executing a motion. A training aid also serves as a baseline against which you can continually monitor and measure your progress, which is vital because even small improvements in how you execute the 5 Simple Keys can lead to large improvements in your game. All told, training aids will greatly accelerate your learning process and keep you motivated, helping you to improve more quickly.

As the world leader in golf improvement, Medicus has spent more than two decades studying golf swing science and developing the most successful and widely used training products in golf. While helping drive PGA Tour professionals to the tops of their games, these products have also become essential in helping millions of everyday golfers reach their performance goals and lower their scores faster than they ever imagined.

From all of us at Medicus®, thank you for trusting us with your golf swing. We're confident that the *Medicus® PureStrike™ Golf Swing* will bring you lower scores and increased enjoyment of the game.

# Glossary

**Address.** The initial alignments of the body, hands, and arms just prior to the start of the backswing.

**Automatic.** Relying on built-in habits when playing golf by occupying the mind with a phrase or song during each swing.

**Backswing.** The first half of the golf swing, which begins at startup.

**Ball Position.** The location of the ball relative to the shoulders at address. It varies based on the motion and club being used.

**Chip.** A motion much like putting, but with a lofted club. It's used from just off the green in fringe areas and very light rough.

**Clubface.** The part of the club that strikes the golf ball. It's controlled by the Flat Left Wrist.

**Clubface Motion.** The movement of the clubface (dictated by the Flat Left Wrist) from startup through follow-through. Golfers use Clubface Motion A, B, or C based on the shot. One of the 5 Simple Keys.

**Clubface Motion A.** One of three Clubface Motions; the clubface opens in the backswing and closes in the downswing (like a saloon door opening and closing). Normally used in full swings.

**Clubface Motion B.** One of three Clubface Motions; the clubface opens slightly in the backswing and closes while laying back (toward the sky) in the downswing. Normally used for short shots.

**Clubface Motion C.** One of three Clubface Motions; the clubface stays facing the ball in the backswing and lays back toward the sky in the downswing (like a pet door opening and closing). Normally used for putting and specialty pitch shots.

**Clubhead.** The solid mass at the end of the clubshaft, which is controlled by the right hand/wrist.

**Clubshaft.** The length of steel or graphite that is attached to the clubhead. It's controlled by the right forearm.

**Downswing.** The second half of the golf swing, which begins at startdown.

**Educated Hands.** A pair of hands that have been trained to consistently produce the 5 Simple Keys, arrive at Impact Hand Location, and know the

111

precise route they must take from address to the top to impact to the finish.

**Finish.** The ending point of a golf swing. For shorter shots, follow-through serves as the finish; for longer shots, the hands go past follow-through toward the left shoulder.

**Flat Left Wrist.** A left wrist that is flat — in-line with the left forearm and neither bent (cupped) nor arched (bowed) — from at least impact to follow-through. One of the 5 Simple Keys and the overall most important alignment in golf.

**Follow-through.** The point when both arms are straight after impact with the club at a 45° angle to the ground. The only time when both arms are straight in a golf swing.

**Full Swing.** A motion where the hands reach a point near the right shoulder in the backswing. Normally used for long shots.

**Grip.** The manner in which the hands are placed on the club; varies based on the motion being used.

**Impact.** The golf club striking the golf ball.

**Impact Hand Location.** The location of the hands relative to the golf ball at impact. The hands are directly underneath the left shoulder with the Flat Left Wrist facing the target. From the player's perspective, the hands appear to be over the toes of the left foot.

**Initial Direction.** The direction in which the ball starts immediately after leaving the clubface.

**Intermediate Target.** A point, such as a discolored blade of grass or the edge of a divot, that lies slightly ahead of the ball on your target line.

**5 Simple Keys.** The five critical alignments your Educated Hands must be trained to produce and reproduce — Steady Head , Weight Forward, Flat Left Wrist, Sweetspot Path, and Clubface Control.

**On Plane.** Having the end of the club closest to the ground (grip end or clubhead end) pointing at your target line. If the clubshaft is parallel to the ground, having the clubshaft parallel to your target line.

**Pitch.** A shot where the left wrist cocks and the right forearm does not exceed parallel to the ground in the backswing. Bunker shots and lob shots are variations of pitch shots.

**Pivot.** The motion of the body throughout the swing.

**Pre-shot.** The period of time before a swing where all preparation ("programming") for that particular shot is done.

**Putt.** A shot played on the green, usually with a putter, using a motion that normally does not move the clubhead more than 2 feet either back or through.

**Radius (of the swing).** The straight line formed by your left arm, left wrist, and the clubshaft that must be in place from at least impact to follow-through.

**Release Point.** The point during the downswing where your hands are in-line with your right thigh and the clubshaft is parallel to your target line.

**Startdown.** The initial movement of the club toward the ball to begin the downswing.

**Startup.** The initial movement of the club away from the ball to begin the swing.

**Steady Head.** A head that stays centered between the feet and doesn't move up or down from address until at least follow-through; one of the 5 Simple Keys.

**Sweetspot Path.** The line on top of which the clubface's sweetspot travels into impact. One of the 5 Simple Keys.

**Sweetspot Pressure.** Feeling the sweetspot trailing the hands via the first joint of the right hand index finger (the "trigger finger").

**Target Line.** An imaginary straight line that extends from the ball to the target.

**Top.** The point in any swing where the backswing ends and the downswing begins.